Family Pride

What LGBT Families Should
Know about Navigating
Home, School, and Safety in
Their Neighborhoods

Michael Shelton

Foreword by Elizabeth Castellana,
COLAGE, Former National Program Director

QUEER ACTION/QUEER IDEAS
A Series Edited by Michael Bronski

Beacon Press, Boston

BEACON PRESS
25 Beacon Street
Boston, Massachusetts 02108-2892
www.beacon.org

Beacon Press books
are published under the auspices of
the Unitarian Universalist Association of Congregations.

16 15 14 13   8 7 6 5 4 3 2 1

*Queer Ideas—a unique series addressing pivotal issues within
the LGBT movement*

This book is printed on acid-free paper that meets the uncoated paper
ANSI/NISO specifications for permanence as revised in 1992.

Text design and composition by Kim Arney

Names and identifying characteristics of some people mentioned
in this work have been changed to protect their identities.

Library of Congress Cataloging-in-Publication Data

Shelton, Michael.
    Family pride : what LGBT families should know about navigating home, school, and
safety in their neighborhoods / Michael Shelton ; foreword by Elizabeth Castellana.
        p. cm. — (Queer action/queer ideas)
    Includes bibliographical references and index.
    ISBN 978-0-8070-0197-4 (pbk. : alk. paper)
1. Gay parents—United States. 2. Gay couples—Family relationships—United States.
3. Lesbian couples—Family relationships—United States. 4. Parent and child—United
States. 5. Families—United States. 6. Gay rights—United States. 7. Homophobia—
United States—Psychological aspects. I. Title.
HQ75.28.U6S54 2012
306.874086′640973—dc23   2012023715

For Donald.
How could I complete a book without you?

Contents

A Note from the Series Editor

The rapid emergence, over the past decade, of the LGBT family from the shadows of fear into the bright light of the everyday world has been startling. Openly LGBT families are now attending PTA meetings, applying for social services, and rolling Easter eggs on the White House lawn. This journey—a continuous, unfolding adventure for many families—has been historically a slow, and often dangerous, one. In the 1950s and '60s one of the main concerns of the Daughters of Bilitis, the first political and social group founded by and for lesbians, was to help women who were raising children alone or with a partner. Dealing with issues of housing, school, being out, and dealing with hostile relatives and neighbors were a staple in their publication, the *Ladder*. The advances of feminism, gay liberation, and the relatively new field of LGBT family law has made life for these families—and really, all families—immeasurably better, safer, and healthier.

This move into the bright daylight of security and safety is immeasurably helped by Michael Shelton's *Family Pride: What LGBT Families Should Know about Navigating Home, School, and Safety in Their Neighborhoods.* Raising a happy, healthy family is difficult for all Americans who choose to do so. For nontraditional families, and especially LGBT families, what should be a joyous experience can often be fraught with social, legal, political, and even medical problems. Are our children going to be safe at school if their classmates find out that they have two mothers? Can I trust the doctors and nurses at the local health clinic to tell them that Bobby's father has HIV/AIDS? How open can I be with our neighbors about the fact that my partner and I just broke up? These are just a few of the problems that LGBT families face every day.

Michael Shelton is not just providing reasonable, helpful—maybe even life-saving—advice here for LGBT families. He is mapping out new territory in helping reshape and rethink how all families might live safer, stronger, and happier lives.

—MICHAEL BRONSKI
Series Editor, Queer Action/Queer Ideas

Foreword

The current legislative battles over adoption and marriage have fostered shrill and poignant rhetoric around families with LGBTQ parents. As the daughter of a gay father from a mixed-race family, I am personally familiar with many of the dominant themes in LGBTQ family issues. In this storm of dialogue, COLAGE is the only national organization focused solely on the needs of the children, youth, and adults with LGBTQ parents. I have the incredible privilege of not only having a gay parent, but also of making my living working for COLAGE and with people who have LGBTQ parents (COLAGErs) all over the country. As my involvement with COLAGE has grown, I have met thousands of youth and adults with LGBTQ parents and I have been honored to represent us within the LGBTQ equality movement in many ways.

COLAGErs often have the ambiguous privilege of being able to hide our identity. We can choose to be bold and out about our families or to be closeted about them, and most of us have had to stare that choice in the eye. Sometimes we make choices that are about short-term safety and security; sometimes we wage love on our fiercest adversaries; sometimes we play our cards close to the chest, fly in under the radar, and confront hate and bigotry in powerful ways. Sometimes we preempt prejudice by being out, happy, and proud of our family in ways that challenge the notion that we have any reason to feel insecure.

On the whole, we are proud of our families. In many ways, having LGBTQ parents is far less unusual than our straight-parented peers may think, but to say that our families are "just like" straight-parented families falls short of reflecting our truth. Much of the rhetoric around our families focuses on the argument that we should have the same rights and protections as straight-parented families because we are just like them: we eat family meals, we celebrate holidays, we go to church. Well, sure, for some of us that is the case, but it's not the whole picture, not by a long shot.

When you grow up in a world that challenges your family's legitimacy, everything you do as a family takes on a deeper meaning. Sadly, many of the challenges to our families' legitimacy come from within the LGBTQ movement. In an effort to win equality, we are pushing the image of the goodness and "normalcy" of our families, we proudly show off high-functioning two-parent home-owning white suburban families who are ready for prime time. In *Family Pride*, Michael Shelton carefully peels off the veneer to counter innumerable myths and misconceptions about our families with simple data. Our families reflect complexity of structure and composition, as do all other families; in a sense, we *are* "just like" other families—in that we just are as difficult to fit into a mold. We are also different from all other families in that we face specific, direct, and targeted discrimination daily. What Shelton captures in this skillful analysis is that our families face the work of raising children in the same challenging world as all parents do, but they do so with an added layer of discrimination, fear, and ignorance.

As children moving through the world with LGBTQ parents, our sensitivity to hostility, judgment, and hate is heightened. We have to search ourselves daily in making choices about whom to put on our family tree at school, whether or not to invite a friend for a sleepover. This is not because we are ashamed our families, it's because of a desire to protect ourselves and our families from the negative (and baseless) feelings others may or may not have about them.

For fear of fueling anti-equality arguments, many of us, parents and children alike, avoid speaking out about the true hardships of living in LGBTQ-parented families. The myths and stereotypes around LGBTQ culture are both damaging to and protective of our families, and their removal is delicate work.

To be raised by LGBTQ parents means countless things. Our parents were often intentional, brave, and thoughtful about how to create a family, partaking in strong communities of other LGBTQ people, all of whom are deeply invested in our safety, health, and happiness. But LGBTQ families must still face hard choices about truth-telling and safety, standing up for ourselves and our families in the face of potential ostracism or worse. We need language to talk about sexuality and identity at ages when our peers may be sheltered from such concepts, and we often have to educate adults like teachers and counselors about us and our families. Some of our families live in four-bedroom houses on cul-de-sacs in the suburbs and have two parents and two children, a dog and a minivan, but most of us don't (most straight-parented families don't, either). Our families become part of the LGBTQ-parented community through adoption, kinship care, foster care, insemination, surrogacy, or simply when a parent comes out.

Hostile environments for LGBTQ-parented families also don't fit into a neat box. As Shelton adeptly explains, the small town in which a parent grew up can be the most familiar and embracing place for LGBTQ parents to raise children, but while acceptance may not be a problem, perhaps isolation becomes one. Never seeing another family like our own is a common challenge for us, but this can happen in a progressive urban environment too, owing to silence and closeted families. The best thing we can do for ourselves and our families is to do the work Shelton is doing through this book—by telling the true stories of who we are.

While our movement likes to engage a certain kind of LGBTQ-parented family in the public eye, there is no depiction of our families so narrow that could possibly be representative or accurate. Shelton's work here reveals this beautifully. Like all parents, sometimes LGBTQ parents need help, guidance, and advice; unlike straight parents, seeking that help can be terrifying. LGBTQ parents carry a fear that their challenges will be ascribed to the unfitness of LGBTQ people as parents as a whole, that their every action reflects on our entire scrutinized and oppressed community. For their children, it is no different; we defend and stand up for our families because we love them and are proud of them, but dare the child of two moms proclaim "I hate my parents!" like any other adolescent would? Not in mixed company, so to speak.

We are far from where we need to be, and the climb is getting steeper. As the questions of marriage equality, employment equality, and family equality for LGBTQ people move from the margins to the heart of public discourse, our families face more, not less, scrutiny, pushback, and discrimination. This is truly at the core of what is detrimental to children being raised in our families. We have told the world loud and clear for decades: our parents are not the problem, ignorance, hate, and discrimination against them is.

A dominant problem in the work toward LGBTQ family equality is the inherent prevalence of the voices of parents over the voices of children. Though we are studied, scrutinized, interviewed, and asked to testify, we are rarely heard. In my work in the LGBTQ community, I am reminded daily that people with LGBTQ parents are not yet located within the LGBTQ movement. In safe schools work, we are fiercely and rightly focused on preadolescents and adolescents at risk because of bullying—but for children with LGBTQ parents, these issues start when they are much younger. Our parents may have come out in their teens or twenties, or even fifties or sixties, but many of us had to learn to talk about and come out about our families before kindergarten. Our parents may have the social agility to avoid hostile and hateful people, but in a small elementary school, we may not. Our parents may elect to put us in progressive schools where our families are more visible and affirmed, but if we are transracially adopted (as is more common in LGBTQ adoption), is our ethnic background visible and affirmed? Our experiences are different, and the work done in this book highlights that.

Although the child raised by LGBTQ parents is undoubtedly a lucky one in countless ways, it is also very difficult to generalize about us. Michael Shelton's book does a tremendous job of illuminating the intricacies and nuances of LGBTQ families while highlighting the simple fact that these *are* families, bound by love and commitment like families of all other shapes and sizes. I am grateful to be a part of a movement that is redefining family not only in the name of full civil equality for all families and citizens, but also with the aim of elevating the visibility and acceptance of all families, no matter their structure. We have come a long way, but the majority of institutions still presume that children live with their mothers and fathers, and whether children have LGBTQ parents or not, that presumption is no longer the reality. The evolution of families reflects a beautiful trend toward creating the strongest possible social foundations for children no matter how unorthodox the family may be, and all families share in that goal.

—ELIZABETH CASTELLANA
Former National Program Director
COLAGE: People with a Lesbian,
Gay, Bisexual, Transgender, or Queer Parent

Introduction

Advocates proudly proclaim that more LGBT progress has occurred between 2009 and 2012 than at any other point in the nation's history. This progress was obvious when, in 2011, the United States and eighty-four other countries presented an international declaration to the United Nations Human Rights Council urging an end to discrimination against LGBTs. "The US government is firmly committed to supporting the rights of lesbian, gay, bisexual and transgender individuals to lead productive and dignified lives, free from fear and violence," declared Eileen Chamberlain Donahoe, US ambassador to the council.[1]

But why then, with all of this progress, did Jon Davidson, the legal director of Lambda Legal, the nation's oldest and largest legal organization working for the civil rights of LGBTs, begin a late 2011 editorial with the following: "I consider myself an optimist. I usually focus on the remarkable progress LGBT people have made through the years . . . But, there are times when the venom and violence that still [get] directed at members of our community [break] through and I find myself shocked at how strongly people still hate us and how far we have yet to go."[2]

Many LGBT activists and leaders have voiced similar sentiments of frustration and disbelief; the more progress made for LGBTs, the more intense the backlash against them. And, unfortunately, families with LGBT parents have become a focal point of this ire.

Signs of Progress

Progress for LGBTs has ranged from the seemingly prosaic (as when the federal government, for the first time, redesigned forms recognizing the possibility of two parents of the same gender[3]) to the phenomenal, including

- The Obama administration's 2011 refusal to back the Defense of Marriage Act (DOMA), which had granted individual states the right to define marriage as they saw best and the concomitant ability to deny the legality of a marriage occurring in another state (thus, for example, a lesbian couple legally married in New Hampshire found that this union was still invalid in their home state of Pennsylvania).
- The belated dissolution of the military's Don't Ask, Don't Tell policy.
- The introduction by the federal government of the Every Child Deserves a Family Act, a federal bill that opens up more homes for foster youth by restricting federal funding for states employing discriminatory practices in adoption and foster care placements based on sexual orientation, gender identity, marital status, or the sexual orientation or gender identity of the foster youth involved. (The bill began the process of debating the issue in response to the patchwork of state rules and regulations regarding LGBT adoption.)
- The Obama administration's directive that hospitals receiving federal funding be required to provide equal visitation rights to LGBT families.
- The increasing number of states passing same-sex marriage or civil union legislation. At the writing of this book, same-sex marriage is legal in Connecticut, Iowa, Massachusetts, New Hampshire, Vermont, New York, Maryland, and Washington, DC.
- The unprecedented media coverage of gay bullying and efforts at the local, state, and national levels to combat it.
- The release of *The Health of Lesbian, Gay, Bisexual, and Transgender People*, a report by the National Institute of Medicine acknowledging the deficit of health research on these populations and advocating for more.[4]

• The adoption by the US Department of Housing and Urban Development of new regulations alleviating discrimination against LGBTs in rental-assistance and home-ownership programs.

The Growing Backlash against the LGBT Community

In spite of the substantial gains, there are dark clouds on the horizon. Barack Obama's election had been predicted to usher in an era of more progressive politics, and the protracted global financial meltdown had led politicians to commit to working on urgent fiscal needs, leaving contentious social issues for future debate. However, in February 2011, Speaker of the US House of Representatives John Boehner addressed a gathering of the National Religious Broadcasters and told them, "I met with a lot of religious leaders earlier today to talk about the strategy, and I think it's important that we understand that what we want to do here is win the war, not just win a battle. And there will be an opportunity some time in order to win the big war, and we're looking for that opportunity." Just what was the "war" to which Boehner was referring? According to Americans United, his veiled comment referred to "several 'culture war' issues [that] are at stake, including abortion, denying civil rights to gay Americans, injecting religion into public education, and obtaining governmental support for religious schools and other ministries."[5] Indeed, the Republican and Tea Party candidates elected into office in 2010—many running on widespread dissatisfaction with the slow financial recovery of the country—were soon engaged in battles that had nothing to do with the economy, particularly issues surrounding sexual minorities. Within days of Obama's edict that federal courts stop defending DOMA, political leaders launched a fusillade of protest against this move and challenged the president's decision.

The religious right is behind many of the social, legal, and political battles facing sexual minorities, but certainly not all. The neighbor resentful of the gay-parented family moving in next door may have no religious affiliation or spiritual convictions but still believe that homosexuality is wrong, degenerate, and a danger to children. This is, to some degree, understandable. Until 1973 homosexuality was considered a mental illness, and even today, some secular organizations argue that same-sex orientation is an aberration and a mental illness. Regardless of the motivation, a sizable minority of the US population is either actively antigay or neutral regarding acceptance.[6] Thus it is not surprising that the sweeping electoral changes arising from the 2010 elections shifted control of state legislative chambers to antigay members, many of whom went to work immediately attempting to dismantle existing laws protecting the LGBT community or write new antigay legislation into existence.

Syndicated author and columnist Dan Savage, creator of the It Gets Better project aimed at gay teenagers, observes that in spite of the progress made in gay rights over the past two decades, clear evidence of this is seen only in large urban areas.[7] And according to activist, author, and radio personality Michelangelo Signorile, the backlash against gay rights by the religious right has made life worse for many gay individuals over the past twenty years.[8]

The current climate for LGBTs was summed up by Joe Solmonese, president of the Human Rights Campaign: "The biggest mistake we could make would be letting our recent successes make us complacent. Stung by our victories, are enemies are lashing out, unleashing their huge war chests to stop our progress and roll back our hard-won advances."[9] Finally, Lambda Legal National Marriage Project director Jennifer Pizer ominously described the cresting backlash by stating, "We may see some new, creatively uglier, and perhaps even less grounded-in-reality arguments than we've seen to date, as there are some passionate antigay activists and others dedicating themselves to the field. It sometimes looks like the desperation of the last-gaspers, but I don't expect the debate to be over imminently, despite how much some of the arguments strain credibility."[10]

The Backlash against LGBT Families

National antigay forces have recently made LGBT-parented families a prime target. In November 2009, the American College of Pediatricians (an antigay group that split from the American Academy of Pediatrics) stated, "There is significant risk of harm inherent in exposing a child to the homosexual lifestyle."[11] The report deprecated the rights of same-sex parents for the supposed dangers they pose to their children's physical, emotional, and mental development. Simultaneously, Exodus International, an interdenominational Christian organization consisting of hundreds of thousands of followers and 230 ministries in the United States, declared that "the intentional deprivation of a mother or father through same-sex parenting and adoption, is not in the best interest of children"[12] while simultaneously fighting against the rights of same-sex parents in legal battles. A *New York Times* article on gay and lesbian adoptions reported, "Adoption has not attracted the kind of attention nationally that gay marriage has. . . . The more it is in the public eye, the greater the chances conservative legislatures will try to block it."[13] And according to the National Gay and Lesbian Task Force's Institute for Welcoming Resources, "There has been backlash against the existence, the visibility, and the success of many LGBT families. Marriage and adoption—two of the institutions which most clearly define our familial relationships—have been the focus of aggressive campaigns which seek to change the laws and even the constitution of our states and of our country."[14]

While some gay-parented families are fortunate to live in communities that welcome and even celebrate diversity, the majority live in areas in which their treatment ranges from indifference and marginalization to censure and, often, outright hostility. Opposition is frequently most evident in the nonurban communities, and every day the ACLU, the Lambda Legal Fund, the Southern Poverty Law Center, and the Human Rights Campaign (to name just a few) report on discrimination, hostility, and violence against gay families in rural and suburban areas. Same-sex parents consistently report their most pressing concern is the safety of their children, who experience a multitude of problems, including avoidance, harassment, bullying, and even violence from individuals, other families, and organizations.

✦ ✦ ✦

After agreeing to argue the unconstitutionality of California's Proposition 8, which outlawed same-sex marriage in the state, lawyer and arch-conservative pundit Ted Olson shocked both anti- and pro-gay rights forces when he went on record saying he was "convinced that Americans will be equally proud when we no longer discriminate against gays and lesbians and welcome them into our society."[15] Similar battles await sexual minorities at the national, regional, and local levels, particularly those who are parents or who desire that role, and it seems that at this moment in history things are going to get worse before improving. Recall that it was only forty years ago that the US Supreme Court found it unconstitutional for states to deny marriages between individuals of different races. According to Evan Wolfson, president of Freedom to Marry, "As people come to understand this is about loving, committed families dealing, like everyone, with tough times, they understand how unfair it is to treat them differently."[16] Inevitably, understanding will come, even if at a glacial pace, and it is the purpose of this book to contribute to the process.

PART ONE

LGBT Families in Flux

✦ ✦ ✦

1

The Diversity of LGBT Parents

A January 18, 2011, *New York Times* article reported that the 2010 census found about a third of lesbians are parents, as are a fifth of gay men.[1] According to Gary Gates, a demographer at the University of California, Los Angeles, who was interviewed for the article, "[A] large number of gay couples, possibly a majority, entered into their current relationship after first having children with partners in heterosexual relationships."[2] In addition, gay men raising children begin to do so an average of three years earlier than heterosexual men. Other intriguing findings from the study show that while there may be a greater total number of queer individuals living in urban enclaves, particularly the West Coast and the Northeast regions, gay and lesbian individuals raising children are more likely to be living in southern states; and that African American or Latino gay couples are twice as likely as whites to be raising children and more likely than their white counterparts to be struggling economically. The article concludes with a quotation from Bob Witeck, chief executive of Witeck-Combs Communications, which helped market the US Census to LGBT people: "The gay community is very diverse. We're not all rich white guys."[3]

Witeck's appraisal is similar to one espoused by the authors of an exhaustive review of research on gay parenting published in 2007: "Most of the research has been conducted with the assistance of lesbian and same-sex parents who are white, college-educated, employed in professional occupations and generally out about their sexuality. We clearly need more research with black, Asian, and Hispanic lesbian and same-sex parents and other ethnic groups."[4] The authors also called for much more research on families parented by gay fathers.

The experience of white lesbians most commonly used in research studies may bear little resemblance to that of African American lesbian parents living in the very same community, let alone two gay male parents existing on the threshold of poverty who hide their relationship from the community for their own safety. While a lack of diversity in the populations used for research studies is one reason for underestimating the true of diversity of LGBT families, it is not the sole explanation. Several others also need to be explored.

The Pink Economy

It is a common belief that most gays and lesbians are well educated and have discretionary money for all those high-priced accoutrements out of reach of the average middle-class-income wage earner (let alone low-income family). Of course being highly educated means they're also overrepresented in the professional realms, and this equates with higher income. Finally, they don't have children, so there are no diapers, toys, doctors' bills, braces, school tuition, proms, and the myriad of other expenses that inevitably accompany the raising of children. If this were true, then one of the perks of having such ample financial resources is that a family could simply up and leave when problems arose. Are you neighbors less than welcoming? There isn't enough community support in the town in which you are living? No problem, gays can relocate. Why stay in Afton, Virginia, when you can move to much more welcoming and progressive Las Vegas? But there's a problem with the pink-economy narrative: it isn't true.

One recurrent topic that arose in my interviews was the 2010 film *The Kids Are All Right*. A commercial success, it also garnered four Academy Award nominations. Same-sex families were proud; they had a film to call their own. Unfortunately, many same-sex parents could not relate to the characters of the lesbian mothers depicted in the film, simply because of the discrepancies between their own limited financial means and the affluence of the fictional family.

Of course, some gay men and lesbians live comfortable upper-income lives, but same-sex couples are also overrepresented in the lowest income brackets. More are struggling to pay off their mortgages (or monthly rent) and utility bills than are sitting at a poolside of their gated community. According to a study by the Williams Institute, one of every five children under the age of eighteen and living with a same-sex couple is poor, compared with one in ten in different-sex married couples.[5] Same-sex parents in the United States have fewer financial resources to support their children than married parents. The median household income of same-sex couples with children is $46,200, 23 percent lower than that of married parents ($59,600).[6] Poverty rates increase when same-sex parents live in rural areas and/or are people of color.[7]

During my interviews, I did met same-sex parents who could afford the best for their children, but the majority of families weren't affluent; many were struggling to simply stay afloat financially. Sadly, I encountered many men and women who had even accepted the myth of the pink economy themselves; they were angry and bitter that they hadn't achieved the heights of success that "most other gay men and lesbians reach."

Metrocentrism

Another stereotype is that gay men and lesbians are drawn to the venues and support available to them in urban areas, even if they decide to reside in a suburban community on the outskirts of a metropolis. But consider the story of Charlene, a lesbian, and Keith, a gay man. They're raising a family together—two boys who are biologically their own—with hopes of returning to rural Virginia when the boys grow up. According to Charlene, "We both grew up in communities right out of *Little House on the Prairie*. I won't speak for Keith (though I know he feels the same way), but I miss that lifestyle. After we decided to marry in order to have children, we recognized that the school systems we grew up in wouldn't be the safest for our kids. We may have been able to put on the façade of the traditional nuclear family and convincingly lie to the community indefinitely, but we didn't want to expose the boys to the homophobic culture that permeated the schools and, I guess, much of the community." Looking reflective, she continued, "So we're living here in a suburban community in which our presence is accepted no matter that we are the most nontraditional of nontraditional families. The school is welcoming of same-sex parents, we have several welcoming churches to choose from, and there is an active gay parent support system. This is what we need right now for our boys, but once they're out of the house and on their own, we both plan on relocating back to our hometown. Living close to the city definitely has its perks as same-sex parents, but I really, really miss small-town life."

Charlene and Keith fly in the face of traditional thinking regarding sexual minorities—that gay men and lesbians can't wait to escape the parochialism of small-town and rural communities for the 'round-the-clock excitement of urban life. But I continually encountered families from the Midwest to the Deep South who were satisfied with their anything-but-urban lifestyles and had no intention of relocating. And some who had left their small-town roots, like Charlene and Keith, but longed to return in spite of the less-than-tolerant climates that awaited them in their communities. Others described their small-town communities being as welcoming as urban enclaves, and others remained in nonurban communities because they simply have no choice.

On the other side of the coin, many families who do want to move to more urban or welcoming areas have remained in nonurban communities because they simply have no choice. The myth of the pink economy mistakenly leads people—both gay and straight—to believe that same-sex families can simply pack up and relocate to more welcoming communities if and when hostility and intolerance become evident. But what happens to the majority of same-sex families who don't have the financial resources to make this happen?

In his book *The Globalization of Sexuality*, Jon Binnie, senior lecturer in human geography at Manchester Metropolitan University, uses the term *metrocentrism* to describe the tendency to universalize the gay experience based on life in large urban areas.[8] Indeed, if I had simply interviewed same-sex families living in urban areas, it is doubtful how meaningful the results would be. In a compelling (and rare) study of nonurban gay life, researchers asked nonmetropolitan gay, lesbian, bisexual, or transgender people to describe the "best" and "worst" aspects of being LGBT in that area and how to improve their lives as rural denizens.[9] The complaints were not particularly unexpected, and some participants stated their intent to relocate to more progressive areas. Some disagreeable aspects of rural life were that the LGBT community was too small, too hidden, too fragmented, and lacking in resources for their needs. Even in communities with an active gay support system, same-sex parents reported they felt excluded. And 45 percent of the participants commented that the worst thing about their rural lives was living in a homophobic climate.

Since the state in which these families lived did not include sexual orientation as a protected group, many respondents reported legalized discriminatory treatment. Intolerance was also rampant. One respondent noted being "so tired of all the people here who come from so-called Christian backgrounds, so intolerant, so un-Christian." Another wrote about a "mayor who allows city councilmen to make racial remarks publicly without reprimand while his wife boycotts Barnes & Noble for selling gay literature." Others described police who refused to uphold the law or assist them once they were recognized as an LGBT. For example, one woman stated she received "no support when problems and threats come" from her neighbors. Generally, many found "that survival within this climate meant downplaying or completely hiding their sexual orientation. For example, one parent who lives in a small town [said] 'I don't want people to know for my son's sake.' Another identified 'the carefulness that is needed when we are in public.'"[10]

These responses clearly illustrate the disenchantment of many LGBT men and women with rural living and explain their ongoing migration to urban areas. However, while 4 percent of respondents in the study felt there was *nothing* positive about living as a sexual minority in a rural community, the overwhelming majority could indeed describe positive aspects. In fact, most offered more than one characteristic when asked to describe the "best" aspect of living in their communities. These included a higher standard of living, less stress than created in urban environments, the beauty of the natural environment, very cohesive support systems, and welcoming and affirming communities. Many did not indicate a desire to relocate, and many stressed their relief that they no longer lived in cities.

Diversity

Gay minority groups have always been present, but their presence has historically been marginalized and ignored. For example, almost all studies of family dynamics of lesbian mothers have utilized samples of white women, with these findings then generalized to describe the dynamics of *all* lesbian families.

We know that same-sex couples of color are more likely than their white counterparts to be raising children. As a startling example, a 2007 study by the Our Family Coalition found that in California more than half of all African American, Asian/Pacific Islanders, and Latino/a same-gender couples between the ages of twenty-two and twenty-five were raising children of their own (43, 45, and 62 percent, respectively), while only 18 percent of white same-gender couples were raising children.[11] Additionally it is estimated that nearly a third (32 percent) of binational same-sex couples in the United States are raising a total of seventeen thousand children.[12]

Across racial categories, LGBT people of color tend to raise children in areas where there is a low concentration of similar families. White LGBT families tend to seek out communities in which there is a high concentration of same-sex-parented families; same-sex families of color are more likely to live in areas with a high concentration of people with similar race/ethnicities, not same-sex couples.[13] Unfortunately, it is the former families, often because of their concentration and the relative ease of locating them, that are the subjects of the majority of studies. There is minimal research on gay-parented families of color and binational couples, and this paucity of knowledge is even more egregious when it comes to nonurban families of color. In sum, our understanding of racism and same-sex families is in its infancy.

Single and Still-Married Parents

Tina voiced her frustration early in our conversation: "You're not going to focus all of your attention on planned lesbian families are you? I'm so tired of hearing about them. Everybody seems to have forgotten that there are single lesbian moms out here too, and I'm one of them."

In Kentucky, one state west of Tina, Chris, a gay father, shared a similar sentiment: "I'm a gay dad, but I'm also married to a straight woman. She's my best friend, and I couldn't ask for a better partner to share my life's journey. I knew I liked other males from the time I was a young teenager, but living a gay life, at least as I saw it back then, was impossible. I married and figured I would keep this a secret."

The earliest research on lesbian and gay parents focused specifically on those who had given birth to their children in a heterosexual marriage, but there has been a perceptible shift: most current research focuses on planned families, those occurring from alterative insemination or adoption. The attention of the media followed a similar pattern. But such families, at least at present, comprise the minority of LGBT families. According to Gary Gates of the Williams Institute, "The places where we see same-sex couples at the highest rates are not oftentimes where we see same-sex couples most likely to have kids. One of the reasons is that a large portion of the childrearing happening among same-sex couples is a product of people having children early in life when they weren't out and are now raising these kids as part of a same-sex couple. This scenario is more common in socially conservative areas, where people are more likely to maybe get married young and have kids and not come out until later in life."[14]

According to the Straight Spouse Network, there are 2 million mixed-orientation couples.[15] Sexual minorities enter into heterosexual marriages for numerous reasons, including needing a "cover" for covert sexual activities, hoping that a marriage will cure them of aberrant sexual desires, and—the most common reason—simply because they didn't recognize their same-sex desires or had kept them hidden from even themselves for most of their lives. Even if they knew they were attracted to members of the same sex, the fear of societal and family stigmatization coupled with expectations that marriage is the responsible sexual outlet for mature adults led many to the altar of traditional opposite-sex marriage. When, and if, disclosure occurs, the outcomes vary, depending on the marriage. Rage, resentment, betrayal, humiliation, and self-doubt (e.g., "What did I do to turn you gay?") are common responses by the straight spouse. Many marriages end, but certainly not all.

While there are indeed planned families and adoptive parents, many LGBT parents are also living

- As single parents raising children on their own
- As divorced or separated spouses still co-parenting with the other biological mother or father of the children
- With a same-sex partner but raising children from their previous heterosexual marriages or relationships
- Living in heterosexual marriages and raising their children with their spouse

These family configurations, though so common, have been eclipsed in the research by a focus on planned LGBT families.

Homophobia

Many same-sex parents with whom I spoke used the word *tolerated* to describe their presence in their local communities; the implied message was that as long as they remained quiet regarding their sexual orientation, the community would tolerate them. To most of us, the thought of being merely tolerated is infuriating; yet for same-sex families living paycheck to paycheck, and for whom the thought of a simple vacation is just as unrealistic as the dream of relocating to an affirming community, tolerance in an affordable, familiar environment is far preferable to condescension, or worse, hostility.

In addition to the impact of community acceptance on how "out" same-sex families are, I also detected internalized homophobia and heterosexism in many of the parents I interviewed; this is not a topic addressed in research because most subjects who volunteer for studies are at least partially out and comfortable with their sexuality. But as this chapter has made clear, these small samples are not representative of the wide diversity present in the encompassing term *same-sex families*.

Occasionally I interviewed several LGBT parents who maintained such a closeted presence in the community that I questioned their mental health. Were they clinically paranoid? This tentative diagnosis became clearer when I met others in the same community who offered a litany of services and welcoming organizations; in comparing these disparate accounts, I was left to wonder if these parents were actually describing the same community. However, these interviewees were rare; in most cases these hidden families were justified in maintaining their at least partially concealed presence in their communities.

I also met parents who felt such hatred for their own sexuality that I could not help questioning how this impacted their perspectives on their communities. Tragically, there are men and women who would change their sexual orientation in a moment if such a possibility existed. I talked to many who had tried reparative therapy and/or religious intervention to "cure" their homosexuality and had resigned themselves to their "condition" only after repeated failed change efforts. Some of these individuals stated they encountered no problems within their local communities simply because nobody knew they were anything but heterosexual; they actively lied about their sexuality or were untruthful by omission in order to convince the people in their day-to-day lives they were straight. Others, in contrast, avoided community contact at any cost; and some of these families were essentially living as voluntary hermits. In their eyes, any interaction risked the potential for unwanted and unintended disclosure of their shameful sexual status. Finally, and for me the most disturbing, were those who were both discontented with their own sexual orientation and who lived in communities that actively rejected sexual minorities. This combination of internalized homophobia and rejection by the community led to mutually reinforcing antagonism, leaving these parents and their children living in shame and relative isolation.

✦ ✦ ✦

Even after considering these five myths that typify LGBT families in this chapter, their true diversity remains uncharted. Mark Snyder, communications coordinator at COLAGE, regaled me with numerous stories of the diversity he encounters in his work. What about the child who has a gay parent in prison? What about the children being raised by same-sex immigrant families? What about the children whose parents demand that they keep their relationship a secret? What about adopted children of color being raised by white parents? What about the children living in rural areas with minimal access to resources? What about children living in families struggling with mental illness or substance abuse? What about children who have internalized their own parents' homophobia?[16]

We know so little. Dana Rudolph, founder and publisher of *Mombian*, a blog and resource directory for LGBT parents, calls for an acknowledgment of the diversity within this population: "So why don't we hear the stories of nonwhite, non-middle-class lesbian moms or other LGBT parents? Many live in states without laws protecting LGBT people against employment or housing discrimination, places that layer of bias against LGBT people on top of a history of racial prejudice. If we have yet to hear their voices, we cannot blame them for keeping silent to protect their families."[17] Where is the recognition of the diverse demographics that make up LGBT parents?

As this chapter has made clear, what we think we know about same-sex parents is not necessarily accurate. Recognizing their diversity is the first step in grasping the individual community struggles they face.

2

The War on LGBT Families

Barack Obama became the first president to acknowledge Lesbian, Gay, Bisexual, and Transgender Pride Month. In a May 2011 proclamation he stated, "The story of America's Lesbian, Gay, Bisexual, and Transgender (LGBT) community is the story of our fathers and sons, our mothers and daughters, and our friends and neighbors who continue the task of making our country a more perfect Union."[1] This was the unplanned opening salvo in what was soon to become some of most dramatic months in LGBT history. Between June 24, 2011, the day the state of New York legalized same-sex marriage, and September 20 of that year, when the eighteen-year-old Don't Ask, Don't Tell policy ended, LGBT people were some of the most unpopular folks in the country. Oklahoma state representative Sally Kern told a talk show host that "homosexuality is a bigger threat to the United States than terrorism."[2] GOP presidential candidates Rick Perry, Michele Bachmann, Tim Pawlenty, Mitt Romney, and Rick Santorum signed the National Organization for Marriage pledge that, according to the American Civil Liberties Union, not only supports an amendment to the US Constitution barring recognition of marriages between same-sex couples but also appoints a presidential commission to "investigate harassment of traditional marriage supporters."[3] Not to be outdone, Pat Robertson, after discussing the Biblical destruction of Sodom on his television show *The 700 Club*, proclaimed, "In history, there's never been a civilization ever that has embraced homosexuality and turned away from traditional fidelity, traditional marriage, traditional child-rearing and has survived. . . . So you say, 'What's going to happen to America?' Well, if history is any guide, the same thing's going to happen to us."[4] Responding to the amount of hate rhetoric being disseminated during this time, Joe Solmonese, president of the Human Rights Campaign (the nation's largest LGBT civil rights organization), sent out an e-mail to members on August 11, 2001, stating, "It's the sheer, unbridled hate from right-wing leaders and national politicians that keeps me up at night."

Solmonese isn't the only LGBT person kept up at night by "sheer, unbridled hate." For many lesbian and gay parents, the political backlash against the strides made by sexual minorities threatens their day-to-day safety and the sanctuary they have created in their communities. For example, numerous homophobic and sometimes simply mean-spirited responses by antigay groups and high-profile individuals follow each step forward for LGBT people, and these occur at the federal, state, and local level; national campaigns against gay families eventually seep down to local communities and feed into preexisting homophobia, heterosexism, or confusion regarding sexual minorities. For example, Michigan's attorney general waged a three-year campaign against domestic partnership benefits and a Michigan Court of Appeals ruling overturned a trial court's holding that public employers may offer domestic partnership benefits. This government-level backlash was followed on the community level by the state's largest increase in violence against LGBTs. As summarized in a 2007 report by the National Coalition of Anti-Violence Programs (NCAVP), "In Michigan and elsewhere in the U.S., these highly visible political attacks on LGBT communities reinforce the idea that it is acceptable to target LGBT persons with violence."[5]

While many queer parents are satisfied if they can simply be left alone to raise their children, at present even this humble hope is crumbling as they experience an inevitable counterattack against gay rights. Indeed, the more LGBT men and women make strides at the national level, the less safe many individuals feel in their own communities. These advances turn the spotlight on many families, and the unwanted attention is complicating their lives, and for some even exposing them to danger.

Justin stands out as an exemplar of this unfortunate dynamic. During our introductory e-mail exchanges, he made it clear he would not talk with me unless I agreed to disguise his identity as well as the community in which he lived. I, of course, assented and, upon our first meeting I naively informed him I would simply describe the geographic region of the country that he called home—the Deep South. He immediately alerted me that even this sweeping generalization was still a source of anxiety: Could somebody still infer his location from this seemingly inconsequential information?

Justin had never planned on raising children and, until several years earlier, had given up hope of even entering a long-term romantic relationship. Then he met Scottie at a Narcotics Anonymous meeting. Justin sensed Scottie was gay from their brief interactions at the meetings, but they did not share too many personal details other than those concerning their struggles with drug use. Scottie was raising a four-year-old daughter and in the process of getting a divorce. When an opening in another branch of the corporation in which he worked became available, he voluntarily moved to this new location to escape the "people, places, and things" of his old neighborhood. Justin was initially crushed when he learned of this because this evidence convinced him that Scottie was straight. Still, over the next several months, they exchanged confidences, revealed secrets, and ultimately confessed their mutual attraction. Within six months, they became close enough to call themselves a family. Three years later they are still together, happy, and completely abstinent from all addictive substances. Yet some cracks have become increasingly evident, not from any issues occurring within their family, but rather from without.

From Justin's perspective, the more progress sexual minorities have made in regard to their civil rights, the more constricted he and his family have became. Every night, it seemed, the national news covered at least one story concerning gays in the United States, and the three that garnered the most coverage were court battles over gay marriage, gays in the military, and gay bullying in schools. Justin and his family felt the effects in a series of alarming incidents. First, Justin was taunted with

"Fag!" by several youth congregating outside of a convenience store. Less than a month later, as he rode his bike through in the center of their small town, an empty beer can was launched at his head through the window of a passing car, accompanied by a shout of "Fag!" Justin didn't know if it was the same group or not. Finally, on the same night that news coverage of the dissension regarding the Defense of Marriage Act filled the airways, the entire family was startled awake when a car stopped in the driveway. Several young men urinated in front of the house and threatened to come back unless the "fag family" left and took their "asses where they were wanted."

Justin had lived in this community his entire life, and he and his new family were living in the very same house he had grown up in and that had been bequeathed to him by his mother. Justin admits he was never "out" and is still not comfortable with his sexuality, yet he had never experienced any mistreatment. There had seemed to be a tacit understanding that as long as he remained "asexual" (his term) in his behaviors he posed no "threat" to the community. Somehow, though, that compact had been broken. Was this because his presence as a gay male had somehow become community knowledge since he had moved Scottie and Emily into his home? Justin knew for a fact that several men in his community were gay but lived stereotypical married lives, but he knew of no other gay families. Or was it because gay issues were suddenly unavoidable? After all, even the weekly community paper covered gay-related issues occurring in the closest city. Maybe it was also due to incessant media attention on gay families? He concluded that it was a combination of all factors. Where once his sexuality had been overlooked, ignored, and considered inconsequential, current events were placing him and his new family in an unwanted spotlight.

Programmed to Hate

A 1954 study of twelve-year-old boys at a summer camp in the idyllic Robbers Cave State Park in Oklahoma might seem an odd item to include in this chapter, but its findings and implications are profoundly relevant to modern LGBT families.[6] While at the camp, the boys were randomly divided into two groups, which were kept separate from each other, though they know of each other's presence. Each group participated in team-oriented exercises, and, within the first few days, the bonding between the members of these two individual groups was solidified. This is the point at which the experiment became infamous.

The researchers arranged competitions between the two groups in which there were clear winners and losers. Antagonism escalated from name-calling and singing derogatory songs about the other group to refusal to eat together in the dining hall, raids on each other other's cabins, and physical altercations. The groups had clearly developed a mutually destructive "us versus them" mentality in a matter of a few days.

Now, jump ahead approximately fifteen years to a related and controversial 1971 study, in which researcher Philip Zimbardo assigned young adult males—all volunteers—the role of a prisoner or a guard in a simulated prison for two weeks.[7] The study was decisively cut short by more than a week when those assigned to the guard role began to torture the "inmates" through such means as stripping them naked, forcing them to simulate sexual activity, and subjecting individuals to solitary confinement.

Both the Robbers Cave and the Zimbardo studies are cited as evidence of the ability of the environment to influence aggressive behavior, but they also offer empirical support as to the propensity of individuals to treat others of a separate group very differently—even if these "others" are in no way different than the majority and/or power-wielding group except for a randomly assigned and purely fabricated label.

Humans have an inborn tendency to form groups. Yet there is a dark side to the group identification process. Research such as that cited above shows that once we have identified ourselves as a group, we likewise identify other groups that are different from "us." As influential psychiatrist Aaron Beck expresses it: "The tendency to place people in either a favorable or unfavorable category has been observed in all cultures: we or they, friend or foe, good or evil, honest or dishonest."[8] Psychological research has found that once we create group divisions, three insidious cognitive processes naturally follow. First, we tend to favor our own group. A second consequence is the tendency to downplay or even disregard the strengths of another group while at the same time excusing the mistakes of our own group. The third process is that out-group derogation occurs when group identity is threatened.

The backlash by antigay forces has caused innumerable straight men and women people to feel threatened by the legal gains made by sexual minorities, and these forces have purposely conflated *equal* rights with *special* rights and privileges that undermine heterosexuality. For example, churchgoers across the country have been exhorted to oppose gay rights on the grounds that church leaders would then be forced to preach homosexuality from the pulpit or face arrest. Additionally, hate-crime laws are decried by antigay forces, who claim that they will force the legalization of practices such as bestiality and necrophilia. The response of Jane Porter of Faith2Action to the 2009 Matthew Shepard and James Byrd, Jr. Hate Crimes Prevention Act illustrates this demagoguery; the act would "jail pastors" and criminalize speech "against the homosexual agenda."[9] While this is not true, it certainly has been effective in furthering the "us versus them" dynamic.

Fortunately, the polarizing us-versus-them schism seems to be eroding, albeit slowly. In 2011, the Human Rights Campaign administered a national survey that found encouraging results: on basic civil rights issues such as employment and housing, huge majorities supported protections for LGBT individuals; a majority of Americans supported marriage for same-sex couples; 77 percent of men said they "could be close friends with a gay man"; and 57 percent said it would not bother them if their child or grandchild was gay.[10]

Still, the pollsters reminded us that "while the country is moving toward equality, it is not there yet."[11] Some of the less positive results were

- Only half (50 percent) believe gay jokes are "never acceptable."
- The nation divides evenly on the issue of whether people are "born gay" (45 percent believe people are born gay, 42 percent believe people choose to be gay).
- 24 percent of Americans believe gay people can be made straight through intensive psychological therapy or prayer.

The most shocking finding was that *nearly half (48 percent) believe they have "nothing in common with gay people."* How different are gays and lesbians from heterosexuals? How different are the families they are raising? The research shows that the differences are negligible, but as will be described below, there is a small but vociferous phalanx dedicated to encouraging the us-versus-them schism through misinformation, exaggeration, and, on occasion, outright lying.

A Historical Perspective

Up until the 1970s most lesbian and gay parents were in opposite-sex marriages, kept their sexual desires hidden, and did their best to raise their children. But as feminism, women's equality, sexual liberation, and empowerment movements by disenfranchised and minority groups rocked the country, these parents, for the first time, saw a glimmering of freedom to live their lives other than the model prescribed by society.

During the 1970s the first psychological studies of the impact of gay and lesbian parenting on children were undertaken. In retrospect, for many readers, the results of these early studies (carried out in the United States and the United Kingdom) will come as no surprise: there were no pernicious psychological effects stemming from this parenting, and repeated studies over the next four decades have consistently found the same results.[12] The most important balm for societal fears was the realization that boys did not become effeminate, girls did not become masculinized; in other words, same-sex parents had no impact on their children's sexual orientation. In comparison with children raised in heterosexual families, those raised by gay and lesbian parents were just as psychologically and socially well-adjusted. In response, detractors claimed that the impact of gay and lesbian parenting was insidious and problems would not become manifest until children reached adulthood. Further studies discounted even these claims but also led to a growing backlash against gay and lesbian parents, which reached its nadir in the 1990s as exemplified by two notorious legal battles.

The first case involved Sharon Bottoms, who in 1993 lost custody of her two-year-old son to her own mother because her conduct was considered illegal and immoral. The Virginia Supreme Court wrote: "We have previously said that living daily under conditions stemming from active lesbianism practiced in the home may impose a burden upon a child by reason of the 'social condemnation' attached to such an arrangement, which will inevitably afflict the child's relationships with its peers and with the community at large."[13]

The second case, occurring in 1996, involved Pensacola resident Mary Ward; she lost custody of her twelve-year-old daughter to her former husband despite the fact that he had been in prison for eight years for murdering his first wife. Judge Joseph Tarbuck explained his decision: "I don't think that this child ought to be led into that (lesbian) relationship before she has a full opportunity to know that she can live another lifestyle if she wants to and not be led into this lifestyle just by virtue of the fact of her living accommodations."[14]

These two cases, while stunning in the implications of their defeat, were also pivotal galvanizing moments in the politicization and professionalization of gay-rights organizations.

Battle Lines

For the foreseeable future, as an *Advocate* article states, there will exist a contingent of social conservatives who are "permanent and implacable foes of LGBT equality . . . They are immune to our stories and lead lives according to the dictates of their religious leaders."[15]

Fortunately, these are a minority; there are far more social conservatives who rely on their own consciences to make moral decisions. Unfortunately, is spite of their relative small number and isolation from the mainstream, this minority contingent—the *religious right*—is well funded, well connected, and continues to purposefully inflict harm in innumerable communities.

The religious right promotes traditional family values along with evangelical Christian interpretation of marriage and parenting. According to the Traditional Values Coalition, "Traditional Values are based upon biblical foundations and upon the principles outlined in the Declaration of Independence, our Constitution, the writings of the Founding Fathers, and upon the writings of great political and religious thinkers throughout the ages."[16] Most such organizations emphatically stress the Biblical nature of their belief system.

These organizations have no qualms regarding their beliefs about homosexuality: it is a behavior deserving condemnation. Leaders of antigay organizations encourage their members to act as spiritual missionaries and crusaders carrying out the word of God. In one of most controversial speeches in its long history of controversy, Focus on the Family board member Albert Mohler proclaimed:

> The scientific evidence is mounting that human sexual orientation may be fixed by genetic and biological factors. Th[is] discovery . . . would not change the Bible's moral verdict on homosexual behavior. Rather than excusing homosexual behavior, such a genetic discovery could lead to pre-natal ways to eliminate homosexual orientation and Christians should support such a development . . . we should unapologetically support the use of any appropriate means to avoid sexual temptation and the inevitable effects of sin.[17]

The American Family Association. Family Research Council. Family Research Institute. Illinois Family Institute. The names sound innocuous enough, implying that professional family-based treatment and research occur in such organizations. However, the Southern

Poverty Law Center, in its 2010 groundbreaking report on antigay groups in the United States, identified these organizations, along with nine others, as hate groups, producing "demonizing propaganda aimed at homosexuals and sexual minorities."[18] All work to derail a hypothetical homosexual agenda that has ensnared the populations of the Western countries and is now insidiously spreading to less-developed countries.

Regardless of their size and scope, organizations that promote bias against gays often champion one or more of the following claims:

- Homosexuality is a sin.
- Homosexuality is a "condition" (either medical or psychological) that can be cured through appropriate treatment and therapy.
- Homosexual acts should be criminalized, even those occurring between consenting adults.
- Same-sex couples should not be legally recognized.
- Gay and lesbians should not be allowed to be parents, including through adoption, foster parenting, and medical technologies.

These organizations are more than willing to offer supporting evidence for these assertions; to counter the rigorous studies and existing empirical data on homosexuality, they offer "facts" about gay individuals as they perceive them. The following is a list of the most common concerns promulgated by antigay organizations:

- Homosexuals molest children at higher rates than heterosexuals.
- People become homosexual because they were sexually abused as children.
- People become homosexual because there was a deficiency in appropriate sex-role modeling by parents.
- No one is born a homosexual.
- Homosexuals are more prone to mental illness and to substance abuse and addiction.

- Gays and lesbians are wealthier and more privileged than the rest of society.
- Gay men and women actively recruit young people to become homosexual.
- Homosexuality is a choice; people can change their preference.
- Hate crime laws will lead to the jailing of pastors who criticize homosexuality and the legalization of practices such as bestiality and necrophilia.[19]

It's no wonder that antigay groups denounce gay parents. However, these "facts" are based on spurious research by professionals discredited in their fields or case studies of children raised by severely damaged parents. No one is claiming that there are no unstable gay parents whose children should be removed for their best interests. This is just as true for heterosexual parents. But, just as for heterosexual families, in no way do the above descriptions pertain to the vast majority of gay families.

These "Family" think tanks and organizations have created a network that is determined to inculcate their message globally. Sadly, they are succeeding, and the messages of hate reach even the smallest towns in the United States. According to former evangelical pastor Jason Childs, who left his church after years of teaching heteronegative and divisive messages, those in the religious right "believe that if you have not been 'saved,' you are living under a curse and are incapable of knowing what is best and that because of this you should be ruled over."[20]

Particularly virulent groups make no effort to disguise their mission as a war against sin, particularly homosexuality. These groups praise aggressive tactics. Consider the words of Michael Brown, author of *Revolution*: "As Christians, we believe that everyone who rejects our message will be sentenced to eternal punishment by God."[21]

Imagine having the majority of your neighbors and the classmates of your children embracing such an extreme religious perspective, as well as the common antigay myths listed above, and you can begin to grasp the challenges of living as a gay-parented family in certain communities. Though these organizations publicly declare violence against gay as unacceptable, intimidation is implicitly allowed and even expected. After all, when the goal is trying to save a soul from eternal damnation, every tactic must be considered.

Not every community hosts a rabidly antigay church such as the controversial Westboro Baptist Church in Topeka, Kansas, infamous for its demonstrations at the funerals of slain soldiers, but many communities are familiar with the "antigay lite" approach now taken by many organizations that have softened their approach in the wake of high-profile antigay-violence tragedies and changing beliefs regarding sexuality. National opinion polls repeatedly find declining rates of distrust and antipathy toward gay individuals, and younger generations are less likely to emulate the antigay attitudes of older generations. In response, high-profile national organizations espousing antigay agendas are on the defensive. Some have tempered their language of hate, while others have taken the opposite tack and become even more aggressive in their efforts.

When organizations have softened their antigay stance, it doesn't mean they are necessarily more tolerant or welcoming; instead they are merely protecting their public image by not being so blatantly hateful. Sue Spivey and Christine Robinson of James Madison University examined the change in tactics taken by ex-gay groups and those that promote reparative therapies (i.e., treatments based on the belief that homosexuality is a choice or pathology and can be "cured").[22] They find that these groups have most certainly backed off on their disturbingly hate-laced language and now take a "love them to death" approach. Homosexuality is no longer promulgated as a vile life choice leading to pernicious consequences for one's mortal body and immortal soul but rather "a condition" that can be treated through compassionate and humane means. With twisted logic, the new gay-friendly agenda taken by antigay groups seeks to annihilate *homosexuality*, not homosexuals themselves, and, in this way, such organizations are able to dissociate themselves from the harm they commit. According to Julie Harren Hamilton, president of the National Association for Research and Therapy of Homosexuality (NARTH), a well-known ex-gay organization:

> It puts it in a different light instead of just seeing it as awful and ugly sin. . . . [I]t takes the focus off the sin and puts in onto the person who is hurting and lets you see them in a new light. Instead of just a "sinner" you now see a "hurting person who needs God's love."[23]

Indeed, many of the parents I spoke to reported that community hostility did not come in the expected forms of violence and outright harassment but instead subtle and heartfelt invitations to explore the impact of their sexuality on their relationship with God. These community members wanted same-sex parents to acknowledge that they were "sinners" who were dissatisfied with their lives. Rarely, though, did they openly malign gay men and women. Still, even a community with an "antigay lite" climate is not a welcoming place for LGBT families and does nothing to deter the perpetration of hate crimes.

Hate Crimes

Despite the strides that have been made toward acceptance, gay individuals and families remain at terrible risk. The violent deaths of Matthew Shepard and James Byrd received nationwide, high-profile media attention. Many of these accounts gave (or sought to give) the impression that antigay hate crimes were fairly isolated, mostly rural occurrences, but they occur even in the most cosmopolitan cities. On October 10, 2010, in New York City, nine young men, ranging from sixteen to twenty-three years old and calling themselves the Latin King Goonies, forced a thirty-year-old man to strip to his underwear, tied him to a chair, hit him in the face, burned him with a cigarette on his nipple and penis, and sodomized him with a small baseball bat, all the while shouting gay slurs. The city council speaker, Christine Quinn, called the event among the worst hate crimes she had ever heard of.[24]

Hate crimes do not necessarily have to involve physical attacks and bodily harm, though this is the fear of so many gay parents for themselves and their children. The federal government defines a hate crime (also known as a bias crime) as a criminal offense committed against a person, property, or society that is motivated, in whole or in part, by the offender's bias against a race, religion, disability, sexual orientation, or ethnicity/national origin. Types of hate crime commonly tracked by the FBI include destruction and damage of property (including vandalism, robbery, theft, and arson), intimidation, simple assault, aggravated assault, forcible rape, and murder. The majority of hate crimes are offenses against people rather then their property, though both do occur simultaneously. Many gay parents whose property has been attacked fear that such acts will ultimately escalate into physical attacks against them or their children.

A remarkable 2010 report by the Southern Poverty Law Center, based on fourteen years of federal hate-crime data, found that homosexuals (and perceived homosexuals) are the most targeted group in America for violent hate crimes. The analysis showed that LGBT people are more than twice as likely to be attacked as Jews or African Americans, more than four times as likely as Muslims, and fourteen times as likely as Latinos.[25] A 2011 report by the NCAVP was even more enlightening. It found that in 2010 violence against LGBTs impacted minority groups disproportionately. People who identified as transgender or as LGBT people of color were twice as likely to experience assault or discrimination as nontransgender white individuals, and 1.5 times more likely to experience intimidation.[26]

Who are the men and women who engage in hate crimes? In its 1998 report *Hate Crimes Today: An Age-Old Foe in Modern Dress*, the American Psychological Association stated that most hate crimes against sexual minorities were committed by "otherwise law-abiding young people who see little wrong with their actions." Four categories of offenders were identified:[27]

1. *Ideology assailants:* Those whose crimes stem from their negative beliefs and attitudes about homosexuality that they perceive other people in the community share
2. *Thrill seekers:* Typically adolescents who commit assaults to alleviate boredom or to have fun
3. *Peer-dynamics assailants:* Typically adolescents who in engage in hate crimes in an effort to prove their toughness and heterosexuality to friends
4. *Self-defense:* Individuals who believe that homosexuals are sexual predators and say their attacks were motivated by aggressive sexual propositions

More recently, Jack Levin, a criminologist and sociologist of hate crimes at Northeastern University, finds that we are now seeing a change in the makeup of hate-crimes assailants. While ruffian, thrill-seeking teens—such as those who assaulted Justin in the story that began this chapter—are still threats in many communities, their acts are increasingly overshadowed by those committed by older sole perpetrators engaged in what Levin calls "defensive hate crimes—crimes carried out in reaction to sweeping social changes that they see as threat to their home, family, religion, culture, or country."[28]

LGBT Adoptive Parents: The New Pariahs

A 2007 study found that an estimated 2 million LGBT people are interested in adopting, yet respective state laws may hinder or outright prevent the process.[29] Gays and lesbians face significant legal hurdles in many states, particularly because they cannot legally marry in those states. Still, the percentage of same-sex parents with adopted children has risen sharply. About 19 percent of same-sex couples raising children reported having an adopted child in the house in 2009, up from just 8 percent in 2000.[30] "The trend line is absolutely straight up," said Adam Pertman, executive director of the Evan B. Donaldson Adoption Institute, a nonprofit organization working to change adoption policy and practice.[31] At the time of writing, an estimated 65,500 adopted children are living with a lesbian or gay parent, an estimated 14,100 foster children are living with lesbian or gay parents, and gay and lesbian parents are raising 3 percent of foster children in the United States.[32]

During the early 2000s, a number of states enacted or attempted to enact legislation to prohibit gays and lesbians from fostering or adopting children, using the same arguments that purportedly disqualified them from biological parenthood. In 2002, the American Academy of Pediatrics, an illustrious organization with sixty thousand members in the United States, Canada, and Latin America, released a report supporting adoption by gay parents.[33] The backlash occurred quickly—several members of the Academy formed their own group, the American College of Pediatricians, and set about delaying further progress for gays and lesbians seeking to adopt. In one of its most cited pieces, the college stated, "There is significant risk of harm inherent in exposing a child to the homosexual lifestyle. Given the current body of evidence, the American College of Pediatricians believes it is inappropriate, potentially hazardous to children, and dangerously irresponsible to change the age-old prohibition on homosexual parenting, whether by adoption, foster care, or reproductive manipulation."[34] Other pseudoscientific organizations followed suit, including the Family Research Institute and the Family Research Council.

There are two types of adoption, and each state has its own laws governing these adoptions. In a *second-parent* or *stepparent adoption*, a person can petition to adopt the child of his or her partner; a *joint adoption*, involves a couple adopting a child from the child's biological parent(s) or adopting a child who is in the custody of the state. It is this second form that has become a focal point for controversy. For example, LGBT couples in Illinois have been able to enter into civil union since June 2011; this new law also granted same-sex couples the right to be foster and adoptive parents, a move that infuriated the Catholic Church in the state. The Church, which runs several charities in the state that place children in homes, was informed it would have to abide with the law or risk losing state funding. The charities argued that they shouldn't be forced to place children in families whose lives don't align with Catholic teaching, namely, unmarried couples. Not surprisingly, the Church responded with a lawsuit. When the state court sided against the Church, the charities transferred cases to other agencies, stopped accepting state money, or formed new groups that are compliant with the law.[35]

✦ ✦ ✦

As the country struggles with momentous societal changes regarding the status of same-sex relationships, particularly marriage, more and more gay parents are finding themselves in an unwelcome spotlight that jeopardizes the fragile bubble of safety that currently surrounds their families. Hate crimes and community intolerance—either overt or of the "lite" variety—are common in the lives of gay families. Certainly, many LGBT parents are out and proud regarding the status of their families, but there are just as many who attempt to maintain a low profile that minimizes risk and danger to their families and lifestyles. The less welcoming their local community, the less obvious these families want to be. Without a doubt, this will change in the future, and LGBT families will inevitably be a nonevent. But that awaits us in the future; currently, societal turmoil over LGBT issues and concerns is leading to unexpected complications for less-out families.

3
Passing

"This may sound so trivial, but one of the most intimidating experiences I had living in Oklahoma was in a barbershop," recounted Will. "I was sitting there in the chair while this very nice older man was cutting my hair. Out of the blue he asked if I had children. There are four other men sitting in the shop waiting for their turn, and some are looking at magazines and another is texting. They're not paying any attention to us. What would have happened if I had been honest? "Yeah my husband and I have two children. Why are you looking so surprised? You didn't know that you had gay men living here? You didn't know we could be parents?" But I lied; I said I didn't have any children, completely dismissing the existence of the two boys we are raising. I prepared myself for the next obvious question, "Are you married?" He never asked it, though. He wasn't being intrusive or even inquisitive; he was simply engaging in small talk. I lied and I hate doing that, but consider the setting and being surrounded by strangers who aren't necessarily tolerant, let alone solicitous. If I had been honest, I know nobody would have said anything to me; the barber would have finished the cut, the other customers would have paid me no attention. But as soon as I was out of the shop, who knows what they would have said? Who knows how far they would have taken this disclosure?"

Exodus

LGBT families are moving en masse from less hospitable regions of the country into geographical areas known to be welcoming; large urban areas are a favorite destination, but increasingly, attractive venues include smaller cities, outlying suburbs, college towns, and even some rural communities. Though still a minority, these families have become a vocal and political force and concertedly challenge schools, businesses, and local governments by demanding recognition of their presence and specific needs, insisting on respectful treatment, and expecting full integration into the community.

LGBT families are following the historical pattern of immigration in the United States: cluster in specific enclaves and combine forces. According to a 2011 review by the *Atlantic*, the top destinations for gay families in the United States are as follows:

1. San Antonio-New Braunfels, Texas
2. Jacksonville, Florida
3. Raleigh-Cary, North Carolina
4. Las Vegas-Paradise, Nevada
5. Providence-New Bedford-Fall River, Rhode Island/ Massachusetts
6. Rochester, New York
7. Houston-Sugar Land-Baytown, Texas
8. Hartford-West Hartford-East Hartford, Connecticut
9. Riverside-San Bernardino-Ontario, California
10. Oklahoma City, Oklahoma
11. Buffalo-Niagara Falls, New York
12. Dallas-Fort Worth-Arlington, Texas
13. Baltimore-Towson, Maryland
14. Detroit-Warren-Livonia, Michigan
15. Kansas City, Missouri/Kansas[1]

Eileen and Gayle, for example, live in San Antonio and know for a fact that there are others in their community who are dismissive or disapproving of gay parents, but they haven't met them. Both are out to their job, their families, and the community at large and make no attempt to disguise that they are lesbians raising their own little nuclear family. According to Eileen, "I remember watching the documentary *Families Like Ours* several years ago and coming away feeling discouraged. One of the lesbian families interviewed explained that even a weekly trip to the supermarket as a family risked an inadvertent outing and then god knows what repercussions. I didn't want to live like that, worried that simply going to a store could lead to consequences for my children."

Eileen is particularly proud that both she and Gayle attend their daughters' parent-teacher conferences; the instructors recognize both women as the children's mothers. This is in contrast to the tactic taken by many other LGBT parents, in which one officially becomes the liaison for the school and the other remains an unseen and unknown presence, giving no indication that he or she is of the same sex. The implicit message is that the parents are a heterosexual couple. Gayle added, "I have a picture of the four of us on my desk at work. If somebody asks, I tell them, 'This is my wife and children.'"

It helps, of course, that both Eileen and Gayle live in an extremely progressive community recognized as one of hot spots for gay families, that neither presents with even a vestige of internalized homophobia, and that they have ample financial resources. These parents and many others have created communities that protect their families by and large from the antigay furor that sporadically convulses the nation.

Less-Tolerant Communities

Unfortunately, inclusive communities are still rare, and most gay parents would be happy at present to live in a merely respectful community. Studies find that community policies and cultural norms are related to mental health outcomes for sexual minorities. LGBT people residing in states with laws limiting marriage to one man and one woman show significantly higher depressive symptoms than those who don't.[2] As might be expected, gay parents living in gay-friendly communities exhibit lower depressive symptoms.[3] Even so, the larger arena of state politics has its impact: parents living in states with unfavorable legal climates regarding gay adoption experienced increases in depression and anxiety.[4]

In August of 2011, the Human Rights Campaign (HRC) began its "On the Road to Equality" project, a nationwide bus tour spreading the message of equality by educating the American public and empowering LGBT people to become advocates for themselves and their families. The twelve-week tour traveled to seventeen cities in eleven states, with a particular emphasis on the Midwest and South since polls found these regions to be the least hospitable to LGBT individuals. Joe Solmonese, president of HRC, stated that LGBT people in such places "continue to face tremendous obstacles."[5] "We're going into the belly of the beast," concurred Fred Sainz, HRC's vice president for communications.[6]

The states visited by HRC were selected on the basis of whether they legally recognized LGBT relationships, had nondiscrimination laws in place, had added a marriage amendment to the state constitution, included sexual orientation and/or gender identity in their hate-crimes laws (or even had such laws), allowed second-parent adoptions, had enumerated safe schools policies, and had statutes restricting positive discussions of LGBT issues in schools. The states that presented as the most unwelcoming for LGBTs were Utah, Nebraska, Missouri, Louisiana, Kansas, Texas, Arkansas, Kentucky, Georgia, Alabama, and Florida. Among these, none had a statewide nondiscrimination law that included sexual orientation or gender identity. Additionally, none had any form of state relationship recognition, and all had passed constitutional amendments to ban marriage for same-sex couples.[7]

Parents I spoke with gave different indicators of living in a highly divided community antipathetic to LGBT individuals and their families, including

- Local politicians declaring their disapproval of homosexuality
- Local newspapers taking an antigay stance
- Public schools (always a bellwether regarding the local perspective on sexual-minority acceptance) actively endorsing heterosexuality as the "normal" and "right way to live"

- Lack of any religious institution that supports gay men and women
- Communities endorsing parades, marches, and demonstrations that vilify homosexuality
- Communities allowing public facilities to be used for organizations that vilify homosexuality
- National coverage of advances in gay rights stories riling up the populace, and, conversely, setbacks being applauded

As these findings pointedly inform us, community acceptance of LGBT parents cannot be taken for granted. Thus one of the challenges that confronts every LGBT family is a determination of just how "out" they can be in their daily lives.

Coming Out

Paul told me of the time in 2006 when he, his partner, and their two sons left for a weeklong jaunt to Florida. Living in Mount Airy, Pennsylvania, an up-and-coming gay-parented family enclave, they had the freedom to be exactly who they were without risk of shame or community censure. But once they stepped outside of it, they felt like expatriates:

> At home we could go to any restaurant and comfortably be ourselves; we would hold hands across the table and our boys unabashedly called us both "Daddy." But once we passed into South Carolina, I felt I had entered an alien world.
>
> We located a gas station and a fast-food outlet at an off-ramp, and once inside and surrounded by strangers, I instinctively felt the need be less obvious in our family interactions—I didn't necessarily sense danger but felt we should be more circumspect. It was then that our four year old dropped his soda and began crying, "Daddy." Gabe went over and picked him up, and he began to have a temper tantrum. He pushed Gabe away and demanded "Daddy Paul." Now people were beginning to stare.

As Paul's experience shows, LGBT parents are often concerned as to how the community perceives them. The glances of others or their obvious stares are of concern to LGBT parents since they may hide hate, distrust, fascination, boredom, and a multitude of other meanings. In a 2007 article, researcher Sean Massey shared a similar experience: "My four-year-old can throw a middle-of-the-restaurant tantrum with the best of them. It is likely that many of the feelings I experience at these moments are shared by parents of small children everywhere. In other ways, however, they are different—they are influenced by the nature of our family (our son has two dads) and the way our family is viewed by the heterosexist world in which we live. . . . I am uncertain whether those looks from others are simple annoyance or something else.[8]"

Coming out is considered one of the hallmarks of identity formation for sexual minorities. Some people do it gradually, while others decide to come out in one breathtaking swoop. Some come out to everybody in their lives, while others are much more selective in their disclosures. Some come out as youth, others as young adults, and some not until they are well into middle age and even later. And of course some never come out to anybody and take their sexual identity to the grave.

Coming out is not a single event. Typically, sexual minorities first come out to themselves, then to their friends, and finally to their families, but there is no one definitive path of disclosure; for instance, some people come out to friends and family simultaneously. People who are out tend to have happier lives, since they do not need to constantly hide aspects of their identity, refrain from activities that might arouse suspicions (e.g., subscribing to gay periodicals might inadvertently alert a neighbor or the person who delivers the mail), and purposely mislead or simply lie in response to even the most innocuous questions. The routine greeting of "What did you do this weekend?" coming from a workplace peer on a Monday morning is fraught with tension if a person is not out and spent the weekend with his or her partner. While colleagues can describe their weekend activities casually, the closeted queer person answers with generalities ("I didn't do much.") or deception ("My girlfriend and I stayed home.")—this subterfuge was given the appellation "Monday morning pronouns" by earlier generations of sexual minorities.

Coming out must occur repeatedly throughout one's life, as it is simply assumed that a person is heterosexual. Some individuals come out to thunderous applause, while others find the repercussions of living as an open LGBT person far outweigh its benefits. Some have misgivings about coming out, and for good reason. And some truly aren't ready to come out because they hadn't even come close to accepting or even understanding their identity. Even today, when LGBT people are far more accepted than at any other point in our nation's history, coming out risks complications that jeopardize and even endanger a sexual-minority member.

The damage may include destruction of what was their closest tie—family. PFLAG (Parents, Families, and Friends of Lesbians and Gays), for example, is known as a support, education, and advocacy group for family members (typically parents) whose children are gay. What is less known, however, is that it is also a second family for many gay men and women whose families want nothing to do with them. These individuals find substitute parents in PFLAG members as they reciprocally assist each other to work through the challenges of the coming-out process. Coming out as a sexual minority can forever damage a relationship with one's parents.

The pendulum has swung to both extremes. Up until the 1960s coming out as queer was unthinkable for most, in spite of the pioneering work of the Daughters of Bilitis and the Mattachine Society in the 1950s. In 1969, the Stonewall riots dramatically altered the landscape, and as activism expanded exponentially in the next several years, gays and lesbians were implored to come out. In 1978, the defeat of Proposition 6 (the Briggs Initiative) in California—a bill that would have prevented gays and lesbians from teaching in the state's public schools—proved that as an organized force gays and lesbians could defeat the challenges raised by detractors. We now even have a national coming-out day.

Reasons Not to Come Out

Daryl and Scott had decided that parenthood was the best option for them and began exploring ways to make this happen. They understood and regretted that they would have to move out of the apartment they had comfortably shared for several years and that they both enjoyed; the addition of a third person, however, would have made it claustrophobic. Thus it was time to start looking at houses to rent. They visited several that were convenient, spacious, affordable, and—a new consideration for the first time in their lives—had a good school. One home in particular appealed to them, and upon a subsequent visit Scott encountered his immediate neighbor. She informed him it was a great neighborhood.

"Do you have any children?" she asked.

"Not yet, but that's the plan. That's actually why we're moving."

"Good. How long have you been married?"

It was one of those moments of deciding whether to disclose, so common to sexual minorities; this seemingly pleasant neighbor had assumed he was straight and married, two assumptions that no longer reflect the reality of modern families. Scott hesitated. How should he answer? In milliseconds, he weighed the costs and benefits of discussing his personal history with a stranger. He opted to pass for straight, knowing full well that if he and Daryl moved into this home, this falsehood would be exposed:

I felt awful the moment those words came out of my mouth, but my gut instinct told me that in this situation I should be less than honest. Sometimes you have to do this just to verify the safety of a situation, and in this particular situation, I'm glad I did. I fudged the truth and told her that *we* weren't married, but I gave no indication that "we" consisted of two men. She looked relieved. She lowered her voice to divulge neighborhood secrets that, since I was straight, I was now trustworthy to learn. I was part of the straight clan. She warned that the neighborhood was changing; too much diversity was being injected into it. She even used the word "faggots" to describe several same-sex-parented families that were now living there. She went on a literal diatribe. Is this the person I wanted to be my neighbor? Daryl and I had to really think about this. I don't usually applaud passing for straight, but on this occasion I have no regrets.

The fact that one neighbor is obviously homonegative doesn't mean the entire neighborhood shares that view. In fact, Scott and Daryl moved into the same area but a different house; within seven years their neighborhood was recognized as one of the gay enclaves in Philadelphia and lauded for its diversity. But would you voluntarily opt to live immediately next to a family that resented and vilified your presence?

Maintaining a secret about one's sexuality is necessary in some occasions, particularly when safety is at risk, but rarely is needed as a default approach to daily life. Indeed, as noted above, there are clear mental health consequences to remaining closeted, including depression, substance abuse and addiction, unsafe sex, romantic relationships and friendships undermined by deception and lies, chronic anxiety, social isolation, and, most tragically, a growing internal antipathy toward sexual minorities.[9] The LGBT individual who can't be out may begin by spouting seemingly innocuous gay jokes and slowly spiral downward to acts of hostility against gay people. Recall, for example, Idaho senator Larry Craig, who mercilessly cudgeled sexual minorities and who used all of his powers to block the advancement of LGBT rights, only to be outed himself. Finally, there is the recurrent specter of regret for many who come out later in life, simultaneous with a sense of loss that they did not live an authentic life.

The decision to come out as an individual is based on a complex fusion of introspection: a burgeoning identity formation, a consideration of the benefits and drawback to disclosure, the long-term and short-term repercussions, and the amount of available support. Certainly, societal trends impact the coming-out decision, but it is the microsystems in each person's life that play the pivotal role. The makeup of the local community, the workplace, the school, and the family, as well as the presence of other sexual minorities in one's life or at least that immediate community influence the decision to disclose or not.

Also, the loss of privilege must be contemplated. Heterosexuals are without doubt an advantaged group, and sexual minorities are unfavorably compared with their norms. Passing as straight not only prevents the possible repercussions that come with disclosure but also opens the door to a vast array of rights, benefits, and even entitlements not necessarily accessible to gay men and lesbians. Jill, a lesbian mother, for example, revealed that she passes for straight in the workplace in order to continue to advance in her company. She was certain that a disclosure of her sexual identity would have put an end to future promotions.

Coming Out as an LGBT Family

As we have seen, coming out is often a necessary, yet often intimidating and sometimes harrowing, process for individuals. Now imagine the process that occurs for LGBT families, in which a multiple of perspectives must be considered, including two (or more) parents and their children.

As noted earlier, LGBT parented families understandably must weigh the impact disclosure will have on their safety:

- Homonegativity is extensive, and it can be blatant or insidious.
- When one family member experiences homonegativity, all members do. Homonegativity, even if directed at one member of a family, impacts all remaining members as they struggle with problem solving, offering support and guidance, and confronting their own personal safety fears. Some families will initiate campaigns to eradicate local homonegative behavior, while others will hunker down quietly, hoping it will pass, or at least not become more threatening.
- Homonegative behaviors occur in proportion to visibility. The more out a family is, the more likely it is that they will be recipients of unwanted negative attention.

To begin, the considerations of both parents must be understood in regard to coming out. After all, one parent can't come out as queer without implicating his or her partner by default. Those in the counseling and therapy fields are familiar with the common relationship pattern in which, ironically, a demonstratively open individual becomes romantically involved with a far more reticent person. It doesn't take long before arguments start, often triggered by an event such as holding hands in public or attending a pride-type event.

LGBT parents also face the issue of coming out to their children. Though every self-help book for LGBT parents recommends that parents discuss their sexual orientation with their children sooner rather than later, for some families this topic is verboten. It remains the family secret that must not be disclosed even inside of the home. Pam and Tish, a lesbian couple raising children, addressed this in the report *Our Families: Attributes of Bay Area Lesbian, Gay, Bisexual & Transgender Parents and Their Children*: "You can't just bring them up as if they were 'just like every other kid,' because they're not. We have friends who didn't talk with their kids about being lesbians. Some African American families don't talk about being African American with their kids, either—but without talking about what that means, they're not prepared. We'll talk about it from day one, that families all look different and that this is your family, we love each other and we love you. We want our children to know something is wrong with other people if they don't understand that."[10]

Parents who avoid the topic of their sexuality—even if they claim to be protecting their children—are implicitly informing their children of their own discomfort and internalized homonegativity rather than considering the negative effects this may have on their children.

From the time their children are babies and toddlers, their presence necessarily brings parents into contact with numerous agencies and individuals who might need to be informed of their family's makeup. Do we tell the babysitter? (One couple I interviewed posed as cohabitating sisters for babysitters.) Do we tell daycare workers? Elementary school teachers? Pediatricians? As these children mature into adolescents with their own identities, beliefs, and values, issues of parent sexuality may and often do arise, even within the most harmonious of households. Sometimes it is children who beg parents to minimize the significance of their sexual orientation and pass for straight.

For example, Jean, with a bewildered look in her eyes, recalled the time her daughter had pleaded with her not to allow a picture of herself to appear in the local paper and most certainly not to expose her sexuality to the community in the accompanying interview. Jean had worked with her employer to raise several thousand dollars for an AIDS charity in a local city, and the organization had arranged for the story in the newspaper. This was a win-win situation for the charity and Jean's employer, but it was a source of stress in Jean's own household:

> I raised my daughter to be tolerant of differences, particularly race, sexuality, and class. It was only when this award came up that I learned she was hiding my identity from her classmates. She told them I was a single mom, which is true. However she left the lesbian part out of her description. I understood she was a freshman in a new school and the significance of peer pressure, and I had no intention of disclosing to a reporter that I was lesbian. But when she asked that I not allow a picture because she didn't want her classmates to see me identified with an AIDS organization, I felt—literally—revulsion. This incident caused me to question all of the assumed rules for our household. How, for example, was I supposed to present myself when she started bringing friends home from school? It had never been an issue before, but high school changed everything.

Jean didn't pose for the picture, and the article mentioned her only by name. She concluded: "I hope when she's older she'll recognize how shameful this was to me."

Another set of parents described truly the oddest community disclosure conundrum I've ever heard of. Indeed, their predicament would make a great television movie. Living in a rural hamlet, they had maintained a veil of secrecy surrounding their family until their oldest son, at the age of sixteen, announced he was gay. He wanted to tell the world, or at least the community that comprised his family's world. His two mothers were flabbergasted; they were worried that his coming out might bring attention to their own relationship, one they had managed to hide from the outside world and even most of their respective families for eighteen years. Equally worrisome, not only did her son's impending disclosure unintentionally aim the spotlight on Josie's nearly two-decades-long relationship with her partner, but it also suggested that they were somehow responsible for their son's sexuality. As Josie said, "People will blame us; they'll say we raised him to be gay. I've even questioned that of myself during the last year. I wonder if *our* relationship is to blame. We're really not ready for this." When I asked her when she would feel ready, she hesitated before answering: "I know this is a terrible answer, but probably never."

LGBT parents worry about the impact of disclosure on their children's welfare. These parents' most common wish is for their children's safety, happiness, and connection with supportive others in the many domains of their lives—including school, extended family, and neighboring families and children. Coming out as an LGBT family can risk dismissive attitudes and even hostility in communities across the country, particularly those that are intolerant.

Minority Families

On April 30, 2011, Steven Goldstein, who chairs Garden State Equality, presented a workshop at the PFLAG regional conference in Philadelphia. He began by discussing recent momentous shifts in both public opinion and governmental policy regarding sexual minorities. He reminded attendees that more federal pro-LGBT policy had been implemented in the 2009–2011 period than at any point in the country's history. He predicted that this "national wave" would eventually impact all states, even the most intractable. Some states in fact were moving even quicker than the federal government, and Goldstein's home state of New Jersey is one of these. In the seven years leading up to the conference date, the state had passed more than two hundred pro-LGBT laws, an impressive record that puts much of the rest of the country to shame. These included twelve expansions of the domestic partnership law from 2004 to 2006, a civil union law, an expansion of the Law Against Discrimination to include the transgender community, a law mandating paid family leave to employees who need to provide care for their same-sex partners, and a law that expanded the state's hate-crimes law to encompass the transgender community.

Goldstein's presentation galvanized a conversation at the table where I was sitting. The New Jersey participants were obviously proud of their accomplishments, but each could name a county in the state that still remained unsupportive of or hostile to LGBT progress. Though the state was thoroughly progressive in regard to LGBT issues, there were still areas that were unwelcoming of sexual minorities, school districts in which bullying of gay students or those perceived to be gay (the unfortunate plight of many children of gay parents) was common, and neighborhoods in which progression of LGBT rights was met with resistance and rebellion. Still, they admitted, progress was occurring and their state was a bellwether for the rest of the country.

As I looked around the room, I was struck by the demographic of the assembly: this was a group of middle-class white men and women. How were these changes in the state of New Jersey impacting the lives of LGBT people of color and/or low-income families living in economically troubled urban areas such as Newark and Trenton? Two speakers had noted this lack of diversity in their presentations, and, in response, the regional president and a PFLAG national representative were only able to think of one diverse chapter in the entire Northeast region. Additionally, esteemed researcher and author Michael LaSala had given a presentation that morning and described his own challenges in recruiting people of color for his studies of the impact of the coming-out process on families. We know so little about individuals and families comprising both a racial and sexual-minority status that it seems disingenuous to boast of progress for all sexual minorities.

Progress is indeed being made at the local, state, and national level regarding LGBT rights and equality, but it is a haphazard and inconsistent progress that seems to have a marginal consideration of the needs, concerns, and challenges of people of color. It is no wonder then that so many LGBT families remain closeted in their communities, however they define the word.

Strategies for Living in a Community

It should be a source of national shame that so many people continue to exhibit homonegative, homophobic, and heterosexist beliefs, attitudes, and behaviors. But as I write, such perspectives continue to reign. As research continues to prove that homonegativity and heterosexism do have an untoward impact on LGBT people, it behooves LGBT families to consider their options. If they find that their community is not supportive but are unable to leave, they need to decide how best to protect themselves physically and emotionally from the inevitable onslaught of disparaging messages they will hear regarding their family or families like themselves. We should therefore not be too surprised that passing as straight or simply remaining vague about one's sexual preference continues.

A 2009 study, *Sliding Under the Radar: Passing and Power Among Sexual Minorities*, asked gay men, lesbians, bisexuals, and those self-identified as queer to discuss their experiences with passing, either intentionally (an active effort or strategy to conceal one's sexual identity) or unintentionally (being inadvertently miscategorized as a member of the majority).[11]

The study found several benefits to passing:

- *Reduced risk of discrimination and prejudice:* Passing reduced the risk of discrimination, verbal and physical violence, and social disapproval. Participants also did not want to be associated with stereotypes or seen as a "pink token employee" in their workplaces.
- *Sense of belonging:* Passing allowed participants to be more integrated into their community as well as maintaining desired and

valuable relationships that might be damaged by a disclosure of their sexuality. This benefit was particularly relevant for African American participants.

- *Fulfillment of obligation:* Passing allows others who are distressed or simply uncomfortable with sexual minorities to feel at ease. Asserting one's sexual identity was seen as an imposition on others. Family settings and religious functions were most cited in regards to this category.
- *Playing with privilege:* Passing can occasionally allow one to benefit from perks accorded to heterosexuals. This was most commonly described by female participants, who passed as straight to gain economic benefits ranging from free drinks to professional promotions.
- *Privacy:* Passing allowed participants to keep their personal information private.
- *Avoidance of sexualization:* This was noted only by female participants. Passing averts the prurient overtures and interests of men who find two women engaging in sexual activity sexually arousing.

LGBT parents and their children weigh the same benefits in their decisions to come out, and all play a role in their own disclosure process. Avoidance of sexualization is a concern not only for adults, but is seen in the musing of teenagers. One teen girl living in Rochester, New York, whom I met at a summer camp for children of same-sex parents, told me that some of the male campers had made suggestive remarks stating she "must be freaky" in sexual matters because of her parents' same-sex relationship. Even when prurient interest is not an issue, being the daughter of an LGBT couple is likely to invite speculation about her own sexuality, as it does the son of same-sex parents.

Living in the Closet

Participants in the *Sliding Under the Radar* study differentiated between passing and being in the closet. *Passing* was defined as an occasional

necessity dependent on the immediate environment as a way of pre-
venting harassment, bullying, discrimination, and prejudicial treatment. *Living in the closet*, in contrast, was seen as a way of life played
out in multiple domains and environments. Those in the closet may or
may not have disclosed their sexual identity to a select group of friends
and family, but they nonetheless attempt to live behind an overarching
straight façade. Both passing and living in the closet are unfortunately
necessary responses to living in a society in which it is still safe to mis-
treat LGBT individuals.

Most LGBT-parented families intentionally pass on occasion, the
four primary contexts being the workplace, religious functions, extended family gatherings, and schools. And on those occasions when
they unintentionally pass, they make no efforts to correct the miscon-
ception. Incongruously, these same families may then head off for a
pride march, a vacation at family pride week, or a potluck supper with
other LGBT families. Passing is a necessary evil to maintain safety,
privacy, harmonious relationships within the extended family and/or
local neighborhood, and simply their mental health by not having to
worry about the repercussion of being a completely "out" LGBT family. This is a message that many gay parents teach their children either
overtly and covertly. LGBT parents predict that the need for passing
will eventually go the way of the dinosaur, but many don't expect it in
their lifetimes.

Living in the closet, though, is a very different lifestyle that counter-
feits a straight life in almost all circumstances. Understandably, there is
not much information on these families, since they deliberately avoid
making their presence known. Those few that I heard about through
referrals or friends of friends almost inevitably became research dead-
ends, since my phone calls and e-mails were not returned. Those few I
did meet tended to live in social isolation, lived in rural areas (though
not always), held strong religious values, and were dismayed by their
own homosexuality and wanted to be straight. Most were not intentionally planned gay families but consisted instead of parents raising
children from previous, heterosexual marriages. Sometimes these were

single parents with sole custody of their children or at least visitation rights. The most obviously recurrent feature of these families tends to be secrecy, not only between the family unit and the outside world but also among the very members of the family.

Nicholas, a preteen male, is one example. He was referred to me for escalating behavioral problems. It is generally acknowledged in the fields of counseling and therapy that success with youth necessitates the involvement of the family. Nick's parents were separated, but his mother was more than willing to do what she had to in order to help her son. His father, however, was less obliging. The mother complained that Nick had become increasingly distant and was particularly unapproachable when he would return from his father's home, yet he had no specific complaints regarding his father. After my cajoling and imploring, his father agreed to meet with me for a private session regarding his son.

"Do you have any insight into what's going on with Nick?" I asked him after our brief introduction and requisite small talk.

He stammered, twisting in his chair. Finally he responded, "I think Nick may have come across some of my porn."

At least we were getting somewhere. And after a few deep breaths, he modified his initial statement: "I *know* Nick found some of my porn. I walked in on him looking at it."

"What type of porn are we talking about?" I queried.

The answer came out in a flood of emotion. Nick had found his father's *gay* porn collection. Dad was a gay man living in the closet. No one suspected—his work colleagues, family, friends, or the woman he was dating. Furthermore, he was committed to staying closeted, and this was the profound shameful secret of his life. The only people who knew were the strangers with whom he engaged in furtive oral sex and mutual masturbation in his health club steam room and sauna; men who wouldn't expose him because they were as closeted as he was. When Nick stumbled upon the porn, this thirty-four-year-old, seemingly insightful and successful man explained its presence with an impromptu but lackluster excuse that a friend of his had stayed in the house for several days. He then made Nick promise to keep it a secret so as not to unnecessarily shame this nonexistent wrongdoer. Obviously, Nick had done just that while at the same time spiraling into understandable confusion.

Nick's father is proud of his ample accomplishments, and he has achieved an enviable level of success in his life. Yet he lives in terror that his sexuality will be discovered. He doesn't call himself a "gay father," but he indeed is. Gay families that are closeted seem to invariably involve internalized homophobia in one or both parents, as is seen with Nick's father, and while it might be easy to maintain the secret while children are young (with sufficient safeguards), their growing maturity and insight pose endless challenges to this goal. Some gay parents expect and coach their children to dissemble or simply lie about their family structure. While they share common concerns with all LGBT families about community safety, privacy, and acceptance, they seem to have an internalized homonegativity that magnifies these issues. These are the families most in need of our help.

Passing and living in the closet certainly have their advantages, but there are also disadvantages and drawbacks. The most obvious are, of course, isolation and an inability to form significant relationships with other people; keeping people at a safe distance limits meaningful friendships, reducing social life to one filled with acquaintances who know little about one's life other that what is "safe" to reveal. Ironically, passing often reduces opportunities to meet straight allies and other sexual minorities who also might be passing. Coworkers or attendees of the same church may be likely comrades, yet they never detect their shared similarities.

In addition to the obvious, a hidden life has other repercussions. First, passing allows sexual minorities to witness firsthand others' unexpurgated and unscripted descriptions of gays and lesbians. Paul, a social worker in a hospital setting, passively passed for straight. He had personal experience with the homonegative comments made by the housecleaning staff. If they had recognized his homosexuality, they would never have discussed this in his presence. Many passing families

I interviewed recounted homonegative rants by neighbors, workplace peers, and school personnel; surely members of these groups would have been more circumspect had they recognized that their supposed compatriot was in actuality not the person he or she seemed. Attending churches where homosexuality was morally condemned—because it was of course assumed that no gays or lesbians were in attendance—was also a common occurrence. While individuals who are passing may glean valuable "inside information" on the people who share their day-to-day lives, it becomes exhausting and dispiriting to continually hear homophobic rhetoric and to recognize the true lack of support that is out there for specific families.

Passing destroys opportunities to educate members of the majority community regarding the misconceptions and falsehoods regarding sexual minorities. Patrice overheard a conversation among neighbors at a holiday event held at the local school at a time when gay news stories filled the airwaves. Several were discussing their antipathy toward gay adoptions. One mother mentioned she had heard that gay parents were more likely to molest their children. Another discussed her confusion as to how any men or women could accept a gay lifestyle; the implicit message was that homosexuality was a choice. Patrice, a lesbian, said nothing so as not to attract attention to herself and her family, yet her external neutrality to these hurtful comments hid her emotions of rage, disgust, and even fear. Others families described far more poignant tales in which they were unable to help out another gay man or lesbian who was struggling because they didn't want to risk outing themselves.

Isolation, inauthentic relationships, silently witnessing homonegativity, and being unable to advance gay rights or simply help other LGBT individuals and families in need understandably lead to emotional turmoil. LGBT families coping with these challenges do not remain unscathed; members report anger, frustration, depression, guilt, anxiety, and loneliness stemming from passing. Most such people I interviewed reported that living a secret life was also stressful because disclosure could inadvertently occur any day. Overhearing a negative conversation regarding homosexuals led parents to days of worrying—what will happen to us if we are discovered? Finally, many reported that their current lifestyle was simply too emotionally draining. Living "on the edge of a precipice" took up too much of their emotional and cognitive energy. Some admitted to using alcohol and/or sleep medications to temporarily alleviate symptoms.

Impact on Children

Abigail Garner, author of *Families Like Mine*, wrote that children of gay parents inevitably discover that hate is directed at their families from the outside world.[12] What happens, though, if this is mingled with shame, fear, and even self-hatred occurring within the family?

Peg is a good example: "We go to service every Sunday, and our pastor always has some negative comment about gay men and women; sometimes he goes on for minutes denouncing us. The whole time, my seven-year-old son is sitting next to me hearing the same message, and at the end of the day, we're both going home to 'Aunt Vivian.' Vivian and I have been together for five years, and nobody knows about her. I never told Rashad not to mention her name, but he hasn't. He picked up from me that this is a secret. What messages am I giving this kid?"

Peg has not come to accept her own sexual identity; recall that gay identity formation occurs in a series of stages, often lasting years. Gay men and lesbians may become parents before they accept themselves. The end result is secrecy inside and outside of the family.

What is the impact on involved children when parents model or actively promote living in the closet? Experts agree that disclosure regarding the family should occur at child's own speed, but I was surprised at how many children hadn't discussed their parent's sexual orientation within the family let alone outside of it—it is a forbidden topic. It is simply taken for granted that one partner doesn't visit with the other's grandparents over holidays, or that only one dad shows up at school for parent-teacher conferences. Friends sleeping over is unheard of.

There is no research to guide us on this topic, but we can postulate the following consequences:

- Children accept that homosexuality is indeed a sickness and a source of shame.
- They engage in homonegative behaviors.
- They maintain rigid emotional distance from peers.
- They assume a caretaking role for parents.
- They tend to develop mental health problems, such as depression and anxiety, due to constantly being on guard against disclosure.

Most tragically, these children may come to believe that they themselves are shameful and that their identity as children of same-sex parents is unacceptable. They go on to perpetuate their own forms of living in the closet. Teaching a child that passing is an occasional necessity is adroit parenting, but teaching that deliberate and ongoing deception is acceptable starts a child off on a very questionable life course trajectory.

When LGBT individuals decide to come out of the closet, one of the strategies they make use of is to distance themselves—emotionally and geographically—from their families. The history of LGBTs is replete with narratives of individuals moving across the country and leaving a bewildered and confused family of origin behind. LGBT-parented families tend to mimic this pattern. Some emigrate to urban areas or LGBT family enclaves. Others retreat into silence in their local communities, particularly if these communities are hostile or parents are inflicted with their own internalized homophobia and homonegativity.

Some LGBT-parented families will always be less than honest about their status either because of their own discomfort or because of the physical and psychological risks they believe are probable. Other families will be completely up-front and never back down or accept a secondary status in comparison to heterosexual families. For those living in LGBT enclaves, particularly those areas renowned for the quality of life for LGBT families, this may be an easy task, but some of the most outspoken parents and children reside in hostile and unwelcoming communities. The majority of LGBT families exist between these two poles. They are not necessarily out to everybody, and circumstances dictate whether disclosure is safe or not.

Coming out as a LGBT family requires parents to first work on their own issues regarding their sexuality by resolving guilt, shame, and internalized homophobia and heterosexism. Indeed, the first step in the coming-out process, the one that occurs prior to disclosure to family and even close friends, is coming out to oneself. As this chapter has noted, development of a healthy identity as a sexual minority takes years and progresses through a series of stages. Some gay men and lesbians become parents long before they have worked through critical issues regarding their own sexuality, and this undoubtedly impacts their relationships with their romantic partners, children, and their immediate community.

4

The Stress of the Ideal Family

The ongoing sage saga of Lisa Miller and Janet Jenkins continues to draw the attention of straight and LGBT audiences alike. In 2000, the two women were wed in a civil ceremony and gave birth to their daughter Isabella two years later, with Miller at the biological mother. The couple broke up in 2003, and Miller was given custody, while Jenkins was granted visitation rights. Miller then announced that she wasn't a lesbian; instead, she believed, she had been coerced into the lifestyle through the mental health treatment system. Furthermore, she didn't want her former partner to have any contact with Isabella.

Lisa Miller presents us with a complicated case of a woman struggling with her sexuality. In an interview with Christian website LifeSite-News, she claimed that mental health treatment staff had convinced her she was a lesbian even though she denied sexual attraction to women. "I think, with women, what I was trying to do was trying to recreate a mother/daughter bond that I never had. When I was seven, I knew how to balance a checkbook because that was my responsibility, and I made sure that the mortgage was paid and I made sure that we had food on the table. I went to the grocery store and things like that. I was always a little grown-up from the time my parents divorced, which was when I was seven. I really believe, looking back on it, I was trying to recreate something that I never had with my mom. It was just such a tangled web because you can't recreate that."[1]

After the couple separated, Miller experienced a spiritual awakening: "I started going back to church after years of not being in a church—I attended my brother's church and I was sitting in the service one night . . . I was just sitting there one night and I thought, 'Wow, I am not saved.'"[2]

Separating from the "homosexual community" included denying Jenkins's visitation rights, ignoring court orders regarding these rights, and finally fleeing the United States with Isabella rather than allow visitation to occur. Not surprisingly, Miller became a hero to the religious right but also an embarrassment to LGBT parents. Her story affirmed the most vitriolic myths regarding gays and lesbians; she was a gullible, naive, and troubled women ripe for conscription into lesbianism by forces promulgating the spread of homosexuality; she had had her parental rights overturned by a progressive and activist court, which had been coopted by the same forces; she had found that she really could repudiate her homosexuality through the power of religion; and, finally, it was claimed, her lesbian partner was attempting to indoctrinate their daughter into a homosexual lifestyle.

While it would be reassuring to think that Lisa Miller is an isolated case, this is simply not true. Carrie, for example, sardonically told me about being raised by her two mothers; in addition to periods of substance abuse, unemployment and its financial consequences, and domestic violence between the two adult women and occasionally against herself, Carrie, now twenty-four, recalls the pitiful alcohol-fueled binges in which one of her mothers railed against her sexuality: "She would be unapproachable and inconsolable during these periods. She blamed lesbianism for the rupture of her relationship with her parents, her inability to find a permanent job, and her unhappiness at home. . . . Of course, once she cleaned up and got her alcohol use back under control, the veneer of normalcy was again in place."

Blake recalls his father (who died of HIV complications):

He was the stereotypical gay man. Every little mannerism and voice nuance you expect to find in a gay man, he had it. He was still married to my mother at the time, and the neighborhood kids would tease me mercilessly about him. I was embarrassed by his behaviors. I remember the fights my parents had. She wanted to know if he was gay. She begged him to tell her the truth, but he denied it repeatedly. "I am not gay," was always his response. He even sat me down when I was fourteen and they were divorcing to clearly tell me he was not gay; this unequivocally was not the reason for their separation. It wasn't until he became seriously ill with his first HIV complication that he told me the truth. He was gay and had been throughout the whole time of his marriage. I asked him why he waited so long to tell us; there had been so many opportunities. I'll always remember what he said: "I was too scared."

Every sexual minority has been the recipient of societal shaming; it is impossible to escape it. The miasma of homonegativity and occasional overt homo-hatred that seeps into a general culture of heterosexism leaves no sexual minority untouched. And this impact starts at early ages. One of the most penetrating studies to examine growing up as an LGBT adolescent was the Family Acceptance Project (FAP), a research, intervention, education, and policy initiative directed by Dr. Caitlin Ryan and affiliated with San Francisco State University. FAP studies how family acceptance and rejection affect the health, mental health, and well-being of LGBT youth. This research finds that families have a compelling impact on their LGBT children's health and mental health, and that the more rejecting family members were, the more severe the health and mental health outcomes for the LGBT youth in young adulthood. Dr. Ryan and her research team identified more than fifty specific parental and caregiver behaviors that express rejection of their LGBT children, and more than fifty specific accepting behaviors that are protective against risk, including depression, suicidal behavior, and substance abuse and help promote well-being in young adulthood. FAP researchers linked each of these rejecting and accepting behaviors with specific health and mental health concerns.[3]

Family-rejecting behaviors include

- Hitting, slapping, or physically hurting children because of their LGBT identity
- Verbal harassment or name-calling because of a child's LGBT identity
- Excluding LGBT youth from family events and family activities

- Blocking access to LGBT friends, events, and resources
- Blaming children when they are discriminated against because of their LGBT identity
- Pressuring a child to be more (or less) masculine or feminine
- Telling children that God will punish them because they are gay
- Telling children that their parent/caregiver is ashamed of them or that how they look or act will shame the family
- Making children keep their LGBT identity a secret in the family and not letting them talk about their identity with others

Studies find that gay men and lesbians recognize they are somehow different from peers during their youth, even if they have no understanding of homosexuality. Yet they are bombarded with messages that same-sex attraction is disgusting, a mental problem, and/or a sin; above all, it is a forbidden behavior. They receive this message repeatedly from family, friends, schools, religious venues, and politicians. Joe Kort, author of *Gay Affirmative Therapy for the Straight Clinician*, calls this "covert cultural sexual abuse."[4] In a 1993 article, Joseph Neisen described it as "cultural victimization."[5] In his article "Illusions of Intimacy," Don Wright named it "sexuality abuse."[6] Irrespective of the name, there is general agreement that this ongoing abuse leads to damaging repercussion as serious as those arising from physical and sexual abuse.

Today's same-sex parents have been the recipients of sexuality abuse in their families of origin and society in general, and they cannot help but bring it in to their relationships, as both romantic partners and parents. The most prevalent emotion associated with this abuse is shame—a belief that one is flawed and unworthy of love and even acceptance. Self-hatred is also prevalent. Is it any wonder then that there are LGBT individuals such as those described in the beginning of this chapter? Many have worked through this shame and only vestiges remain; for others, though, it is a continual presence haunting the fringes of their lives.

On June 20, 2011, I spoke to Jennifer Chrisler, executive director of the Family Equality Council, an organization that works at all levels of government to advance full social and legal equality on behalf of sexual minorities raising children. She observed that the research on same-sex parents struggling with their own childhood sexuality abuse and internalized homonegativity is nonexistent. However, she has sufficient anecdotal evidence to know that the effect on their own children is "significant and profound."[7] At the time of our conversation, there were still thirty-eight states that permitted employers to terminate workers on the basis of sexuality, a powerful reason for parents to collude with children to keep their family's status a secret. This might not be the healthiest agreement, but when one's very livelihood is at risk, it makes sense. Children can cope with this charade when parents are open about their concerns, explain the reason for the machination, and continually discuss the obstacles this presents in a child's life.

Others parents, though, conspire to keep their sexuality a taboo even with the children they live with; these parents have created their own Don't Ask, Don't Tell policy. Glenn, for example, didn't realize his mother and "aunt" were actually lovers until he was a teenager:

> I knew she wasn't a [biological] aunt, because I knew all my mother's siblings. I thought she was a close friend, and "aunt" was just a sign of respect. We lived in a small apartment, so it made sense that they shared the same bedroom. And because she wasn't family, it made perfect sense that "Aunt Ginny" didn't join us on holidays and birthdays at my mother's relatives. I even remember my mother telling her sister that Ginny lived with us in order to help pay the rent. I was thirteen before I even questioned [this], and that was simply because a friend thought our living arrangement was odd. When I told my mother, she testily told me that my friend didn't know what he was talking about. Even then she didn't come out and simply tell me the truth.

The Facade of the Perfect Family

In 1977, Florida's Dade County passed an ordinance that banned discrimination in areas of housing, employment, and public accommodation based on sexual orientation. Foes (fronted by Anita Bryant and her Save Our Children organization) massed for a counterassault, which included the release of a television advertisement that is still considered one of the most effective pieces of antigay propaganda ever created. In the words of Fred Fejes, author of *Gay Rights and Moral Panic*:

> It opened with film footage of the nationally televised (and hosted by Bryant) Miami Orange Bowl Parade; "Miami's gift to the nation– wholesome entertainment," the announcer intones. "But in San Francisco when they take to the streets, it's a parade of homosexuals." Using film footage provided by the San Francisco Deputy Sheriffs Association, the picture turned to scenes of from the San Francisco's Gay Pride parade with half-naked men in leather kissing and drag queens dancing, with the voice-over continuing, "men hugging other men, cavorting with little children, wearing dresses and make-up." The voice-over concluded, "The same people who turned San Francisco into a hotbed of homosexuality want to do the same in Florida," and it urged viewers to vote against the ordinance.[8]

The LGBT community's concern with public image didn't begin in the 1970s; the vanguard of gay rights understood public image was a tinderbox. Franklin Kameny, an astronomer who was fired from his position with the federal government for his homosexuality in 1957, organized the first public demonstrations in the United States demanding fair treatment for sexual minorities. These were held in 1965 at both the Liberty Bell site in Philadelphia and the White House. Kameny required that demonstrators adhere to a strict dress code: men in shirts and ties and women in dresses. He recognized the importance of public image, and the battle over this image continues today, influencing same-sex parents and their families. Out families must adhere to a metaphorical dress code: they must be model families.

The LGBT community tends to promote upbeat and positive images of gay and lesbian families. For example, a *New York Times* story on the growing number of same-sex parent adoptions in the United

States focuses on Matt and Ray Lees, who have adopted eight children, including five siblings. As Matt Rees notes: "It was the best way we could think of spending the next 20 years of our lives."[9] Yes, Matt and Ray have occasional odd looks from neighbors but otherwise are a satisfied, out, and successful family.

The story of the two college-educated and successful Leeses is a stark contrast to the saga of Lisa Miller, but the reality is that there are innumerable other Lisa Millers existing in the community of same-sex parents, male and female. Hidden or closeted families may purposefully attempt to minimize outside involvement, since any intrusion may inadvertently divulge the secret of their identity. According to Sue Hyde, longtime LGBT activist and author of *Come Out and Win*, "While our movement has forcefully and critically refuted the categorical smears of criminality of adult sexuality and mental illness . . . [they] craft organizing materials and events that feature only the most wholesome (i.e., acceptable to the mainstream) aspects of the LGBT community, censor the more colorful characters in the LGBT communities, and, most recently, heavily promote our own population of gay- and lesbian-headed families."[10]

What are the images the LGBT community want the public to see in regards to same-sex parents? Hyde is unassailably correct when she states that there is a focus on "wholesome" families. We don't see the families who are struggling and who have serious issues; to even acknowledge these families is to fuel stereotypes that LGBT parents are not fit to raise children. For example, it is now understood that family involvement is optimal for the treatment of substance abuse and addiction; a struggling LGBT parent who is in the closet will forgo family intervention or simply lie about his or her family. If a child in these families develops an abuse or addiction disorder, the dilemma is even more complicated. Jessica admitted with shame that she had conspired with her fourteen-year-old daughter Michelle to keep their family a secret from a counselor: "It was mortifying to listen to this counselor telling us about the impact of family dynamics on Michelle's drug problem, yet the entire time we're sitting there we're lying to him—I'm pretending to be a single mom instead of talking about Jody [her girl-friend] and her ongoing alcohol abuse in our home." Jessica and her family live in a small town in West Virginia (Jessica called it a "hamlet") and they had to drive more than an hour to even obtain treatment services. Even more intimidating, the facility was Christian-based and not going to look upon her family with respect. Jessica summarized her dilemma with a barely discernible shrug: "What could I do?"

Out families experience another dilemma: they must hide their problems. Like any other family, same-sex-parented families are not perfect. Yet, unlike straight-parented families, they are expected to be—they must certainly live as though they are. In spite of the abundance of research proving that children are both physically and mentally healthy in same-sex families, LGBT parents must still battle demeaning and dangerous myths that abound regarding them and their parenting abilities (e.g., they are child molesters; they will indoctrinate children into homosexuality). It is not surprising that sexual-minority parents have had to go to the opposite extreme to counter these pernicious depictions; they must present as perfect families (or as near as possible to this ideal), no matter the reality of their lives.

Same-sex parents and their families receive higher scrutiny than traditional families, are held to a higher standard, and must continually be on their best behavior in the public eye. In *Families Like Mine*, Abigail Garner refers to "straight family privilege." She pleads that "LGBT families should be allowed to be just as wacky, troubled, or complex as any other American family."[11] Unfortunately the privilege of showing the less positive aspects of same-sex family life is not granted to all families. Certainly the majority of families, gay or straight, don't want to air their "dirty laundry" and would rather keep such information within the walls of the home; yet straight families coping with domestic violence, drug abuse, sexual abuse, and mental illness receive societal support. Neighbors, families, teachers, medical professions, and even politicians don't blame these problems on the parents' sexuality. But if a same-sex parent experiences the same problems, these same people will often look at sexuality as the pivotal factor in causing all these behaviors.

Thus the recommendation of Timothy Biblarz and Evren Savci of the Department of Sociology of the University of Southern California was refreshing. In their exhaustive 2010 review of the research literature on LGBT families, they reported that researchers were disinclined to address controversial topics relevant to gay families, such as abuse, break up rates, and inequalities between partners so as not to give anti-LGBT forces additional fodder. They recommended engaging in this research, since it "could serve the community" and, in the end, "outweigh worrying too much about what antigay advocates might latch onto from the literature."[12]

Starting at Home

A cardinal rule in LGBT-parented families: *The less respectful and safe the outside world, the safer the sanctuary of the family must be.*

Adrienne recalls her childhood with a sense of bemusement and detachment:

One of the most vivid memories I have of my fathers [one was her maternal uncle Bill, who had assumed custody of her after her mother died] was our trip back from [a world-famous theme park]. I was probably six or seven at the time. I was in the backseat and I could tell they were furious at each other, but not a word was said. There was just silence; they wouldn't even turn on the radio. We pulled into a rest stop off the interstate, and Adam went into the use the bathroom. Uncle Bill pulled off; he just drove us back onto the highway and left Adam there—stranded. We were hundreds of miles from home. This was how they fought. It wasn't until years later that I learned Adam had a compulsive sexual problem in addition to his drinking, which was already well known to me. I can only conjecture to what he did on that trip that so infuriated Uncle Bill. They fought and fought all the time, and this meant physically fighting. Both had a temper, but Uncle Bill's was the worse. Looking back, a lot of times I felt safer in school then I did at home.

Connie, whom I met briefly at a Pride Festival, shared some memories of her childhood:

> I thought my mothers were the height of hypocrisy. They let everybody know that they were same-sex parents; the entire neighborhood knew, including my school. They refused to back down to anyone, and for that I'm glad; this taught me a lot. My friends would always tell me my moms were "so cool." But I never brought them home. No way. If Phyllis was drinking, which was most days of the week, I could never tell what to expect. The slightest provocation would send her off into a rage. She hit me, but Shirley got it far worse than I did. Did I live in a house with domestic violence? Yes I did. Instead of presenting as the perfect out and proud family who would go head-to-head with any source of discrimination, I really wish my moms had extended a little more energy on making the *inside* of our house safe. I didn't grow up feeling safe because of what happened inside of my home rather that what happened *outside* of it.

Future generations of LGBT-parented families will have several past generations of examples to emulate (in addition to learning from their mistakes). This is not true for the current generation of same-sex parents, most of who are learning as they go along to work through the challenges of being both a parent and a sexual minority. Families facing an ambivalent or hostile social environment often create a dynamic in which the connections between family members are overly close and thus limit individual growth and independence. Problems become particularly obvious when developing children begin to try to assert some measure of autonomy in seeking a life beyond the family. As described by psychologist Joanna Bunker Rohrbaugh, "Community rejection leads partners to cling to each other in an attempt to shut out the rejecting, homophobic world; this coping strategy seeks to develop and protect the sense of stability and permanence that our culture enhances in heterosexual relationships but . . . The social isolation caused by secrecy can contribute to difficulties with boundaries and differentiation."[13]

Problems within the family can occur between two parents, between a parent (or parents) and a child, and between children. The most common issues leading to family fracture are substance abuse, financial stress, sexual concerns, mental illness, domestic violence, and communication problems.

Coming Out to One's Children

Parents may go to great lengths to present as heterosexual for their children, or at least downplay their homosexuality. Some even embrace asexual lifestyles. Secrets take root, topics become unapproachable, and children grow up in an atmosphere of confusion. Not only does this damage to the parent/child relationship, but these children may well have problems in their own relationships as they mature.

Families struggling with parental substance abuse are exemplars of the pernicious effects of keeping family secrets. All members of a family are well aware that mom or dad has a drug or alcohol problem and attempt to live their lives around the issue; the phrase *pretend normal* is often used to describe this dynamic. According to the National Association for Children of Alcoholics:

> Families have a remarkable ability to maintain what family therapists call homeostasis. When alcohol or drugs are introduced into a family system, the family's ability to self-regulate is challenged . . . Such families often become characterized by a kind of emotional and psychological constriction, where no one feels safe to express their authentic selves for fear of triggering a disaster; their genuine feelings are often hidden under strategies for keeping safe, like pleasing or withdrawing. The family becomes organized around trying to manage the unmanageable disease of addiction.[14]

The same dynamic can be applied to families struggling with issues of sexuality. Shame about sexuality will inevitably percolate down to children. Parents who refuse to discuss their sexuality or go to the extent of hiding it are giving a clear message that homosexuality is indeed shameful. Samuel, a nineteen-year-old man I work with in a clinical setting, has still not broached his father's sexuality. Samuel has been indoctrinated with societal depictions of gay men as an out-of-control, sexually voracious group passing diseases from one person to another. He had seen movies such as *The Dilemma*, in which the typical insult was to call someone or something "gay," and *The Hangover*, in which for comedic effect one actor calls out, "Paging Dr. Faggot!" Samuel was aware of the controversy over comedian Tracy Morgan's statement that he would stab his son if he acted gay (and this was supposed to get laughs). Still, his father—who under the guise of being a single man, engaged in furtive sex with men while occasionally dating women to throw his parents and family off track—refused to discuss his sexuality with his only son. Sam's father was ashamed of his own sexuality. Should we then expect Sam to celebrate his father's sexuality?

I recall a dismaying conversation I had with an eighteen-year-old staff member of Mountain Meadow camp, the first camp in the United States for children of same-sex parents. He admitted envying several campers who had arrived days earlier. They were regaling the entire camp community of their experiences at Family Week in Provincetown, Massachusetts, an event that had ended just prior to the first day of camp. Carl told me that he and his sister knew their mothers were lesbian, but that it was a verboten topic. Even though it had never been suggested, he instinctively knew never to bring friends over to the house or discuss his family in depth. He summed up his childhood as one filled with secrecy. And most regretfully, he stills feels a sense of shame regarding his own status as the child of same-sex parents.

In contrast, Kerry did tell her children she was sexually attracted to other women (she did not use the word *lesbian*). I asked her how her teenage girls had responded. "Very well," she replied. "They haven't asked any questions about it, so it's not a topic we discuss very much." There is no doubt that a parent's revelation of his or her sexuality status has an impact on teenagers; even if they say very little, their silence does not connote acceptance. This book has already made it clear that coming out is not a one-time event, and this applies to disclosure to one's children. As a comparison, no responsible parents would inform their children that they are divorcing and then neglect to address the issue at any further point. Children need time to process an important revelation; some will respond immediately with a barrage of questions, while others will lapse into silence in order to contemplate the news and its impact. A "hit and run" disclosure to children is more likely to be due to parental fears and internalized homophobia rather than consideration for the best interests of the children.

Some same-sex parents I have spoken to told me they are indeed out to their children when in fact they haven't actually done the hard work of processing the meaning of this for each child and the family as a whole. Coming out to one's children requires much more than saying, "I'm gay" or "I'm lesbian." In the parenting resource "Talking to Children About Our Families," we are reminded, "Assuming that children who don't ask questions don't have questions may lead to children thinking that there is a need for or expectation of silence about their families."[15] And as the COLAGE organization reminds us, "It's never too early to come out to your child/ren. Kids understand love. What they don't understand is deception or hiding. And it's never too late to come out to your child. COLAGE has met folks in their forties whose parents are just now coming out to them. A lot of mysteries are being solved, and missing puzzle pieces falling into place for these families. Often knowing the truth will be a relief for kids of all ages."[16]

Family homeostasis that develops due to family secrets works in the short-term, but the long-term consequences are regrettable. When parents hide their sexuality from children, it only damages the parents themselves, children, and the family in general as the years pass.

Immersion

As described above, coming out and developing a positive identity is a process that takes time, longer for some than for others. One stage that many sexual minorities pass through is called the *immersion* stage, so named because during this stage LGBTs immerse themselves in the sexual-minority subculture, surrounding themselves with everything gay and eschew and even denigrate straight culture. Though almost all sexual minorities pass through this stage, it can nevertheless lead to difficulties, including impacting their children. Keitha, for example, is worried about her teenage son's response to her sexual identity: "I am proud that my son is so supportive of me, but I'm beginning to worry that he's not as—I want to use the right word here—he's not well-rounded. He knows more about gay and lesbian history than I do even now. His only friends are the kids of other same-sex marriages. He works at a gay-owned business and is hip to what's going on in the sexual-minority culture. But he's not gay, and he seems to have a grudge against the straight world."

According to researchers Dana Finnegan and Emily McNally, many gays and lesbians in this stage "are likely to dehumanize heterosexuals (for example, call them 'breeders') and view the straight world as inferior (e.g., insensitive, power-hungry, cruel). These actions are part of a complete or partial withdrawing from mainstream; a splitting of the world into us and them." People in this stage "tend to experience two major feeling states—pride bordering on arrogance and great anger."[17] Sandra Anderson, researcher of behavioral issues for sexual minorities, observes that during this stage, "There is immersion in the lesbian/gay culture and association primarily with gay/lesbian people. There is growing anger with the dominant, oppressive, heterosexual culture."[18] Renowned clinician Joe Kort agrees, noting that in this stage sexual minorities "do not distinguish between straight people who are heterosexist or homophobic and those who are not. All of their previous repression in now explosively directed outward . . . They devour gay books, magazines, and weeklies, absorbing all the culture's earmarks and trademarks. Disdain for the straight world surfaces; they tend to think it's 'them against us.'"[19]

Keitha also recognized her son was receiving messages of intolerance in his workplace. Both his boss and coworkers (all gay men) belittled heterosexuals as "breeders" and expressed ambivalence and, sometimes, disgust toward the majority population. It didn't matter that much of this wasn't meant to be taken seriously, particularly since her son was known to be straight. Yet intolerance in any form is not acceptable to Keitha: "As a lesbian in the South, I struggled; let there be no doubt of that. I was married with a child before I even knew what lesbianism was. My father disowned me for more than a decade. So I did have animosity with the straight world. But now I work in a hospital with zero tolerance for discrimination. I have a boss who is straight man who simply adores me. I have straight and gay friends. There are both good and bad aspects to the gay and lesbian world just as much as the straight world. But a meaningful life requires living in both worlds and fighting for positive change in *both worlds*."

Keitha had a private conversation with her son's boss, asking him to tone down the intolerance in the workplace, no matter how facile it was meant to be. She is also openly critical in front of her son of questionable decisions in both straight and gay politics. She has straight men and women over as part of a monthly game night. But the one area of her life in which she feels she is most actively a role model is in her relationship with her family: "I make concessions to my father and sister so that we can have a relationship. My son thinks I should force my sexuality in their faces, but the result is that we will again have no relationship. In their presence I make concessions."

Sexual minorities have every reason to feel resentment and anger for the way they have been treated in the past and for the stigmatization that are still subjected to today. But many LGBT folks ultimately emerge from their oversimplified, either/or view of the world and integrate into the wider community. They become less militant and recognize that while there are heterosexist and homophobic straights, allies also exist. Children should be angry if they and their parents are treated as pariahs and second-class citizens, but the development of an us-versus-them mentality only fosters an unnecessary hatred. There are innumerable straight allies out there, and choosing to ignore, avoid, or devalue them is a risk.

PART TWO

The Challenges Confronting LGBT Families

✦ ✦ ✦

5
Schools

Imagine the concerns of same-sex families with children in the Midland School District in Arkansas. In October 2010, the vice president of the district, Clint McCance, responded to requests for students to wear purple in the wake of the nationally reported spate of gay teenage suicides by writing, "Seriously they want me to wear purple because five queers killed themselves. The only way im wearin it for them is if they all commit suicide. I cant believe the people of this world have gotten this stupid. We are honoring the fact that they sinned and killed thereselves because of their sin. REALLY PEOPLE [Author's note: Spelling and punctuation from the original]."[1] The outpouring of public revulsion at his comments eventually led to his emotional apology and resignation during a television appearance. A year later, a similar scene played out in New Jersey. In October 2011, New Jersey teacher Vicki Knox posted a hateful diatribe against LGBTs: "Homosexuality is a perverted spirit that has existed from the beginning of creation. The word of God refers to it often. That's if you believe the Word to be truly God's intended blueprint for his people. I have friends and loved ones who are practicing/living as homosexuals. Yes I love can care about them. We hug and exchange gifts. We have family dinners. But how they live and their actions, behaviors—CHOICES are against the nature and character of God! . . . I know sin and it breeds like cancer!"[2] The governor of the state quickly denounced her, and the Human Rights Campaign initiated a letter-writing campaign to the local school board. Simultaneously, social conservatives groups rallied to her cause; the National Organization for Marriage, for example, labeled her a "Christian martyr."[3]

While lesbian and gay parents were no doubt reassured by the national condemnation McCance and Knox received, these incidents also spotlighted a problem that is rife in schools across the country: students, teachers, and other school personnel can and do subvert efforts to make schools safe for all youth, including the children of LGBT parents.

The School Experiences of Children of LGBT Parents

Much of what we know about the school experiences of children of LGBT parents comes from anecdotal reports and a small number of studies. For example, a 2008 meta-analysis of nineteen studies examining developmental outcomes for LGBT-parented youth found, "Children raised by gay or lesbian parents face a number of challenges in the classroom. First, many teachers are not well educated on same-sex relationships and school administrators are reluctant to discuss the issue. Second, many prospective teachers hold negative views toward gay and lesbian individuals, potentially adversely affecting the relationships these teachers will have with sexual-minority students and families. Third, teachers are not likely to initiate a safe and welcoming environment for gay and lesbian students or their parent(s)."[4]

The most exhaustive resource is *Involved, Invisible, Ignored,* a 2008 study published by the Gay, Lesbian, and Straight Education Network (GLSEN) that explores the experiences of LGBT parents and children in US public schools. Half of all the students in the study reported feeling unsafe in school, and the most commonly offered reason was having an LGBT parent; 40 percent reported they had been verbally harassed in school because of their family; 38 percent reported being verbally harassed in school because of their actual or perceived sexual orientation (even though the vast majority of respondents identified themselves as heterosexual); and 12 percent reported they had been physically harassed or assaulted in the past year because they had LGBT parents. Nearly a quarter of students had been mistreated by or received negative comments from the parents of other students specifically because they had an LGBT parent. Finally, 11 percent of students reported being directly mistreated by a teacher, and 15 percent heard negative comments by teachers.[5] Children of LGBT parents are also made to feel excluded in schools. One student reported, "When people and our teacher talk about LGBT people in class and everyone laughs because they think it's gross or something, I feel uncomfortable because I'm the only one not laughing. It's like there [sic] making fun of me in a way."[6] More than 30 percent of students in the study reported feeling that they could not fully participate in school specifically because they had an LGBT parent, and 36 percent felt that school personnel did not acknowledge that they were from an LGBT family. In addition, about a fifth of students reported that they had been discouraged from talking about their parents or family at school by a teacher, principal, or other school staff person. Consider this comment from an eleventh grader: "In Spanish [class], we were doing a project that involved describing our home and introducing our family. I talked to my teacher and explained my situation, and she said it would be better for me to say I had a single mother and not mention her partner at all. It made me mad, so I made a point of including my other mom, and I ended up failing the project."[7] And a ninth grader reported, "We had a dance team banquet and we were supposed to have our parents come, but our directors said it would be better if I only brought one of my moms so I would not cause a disruption."[8]

Students in the study observed that the three most common sources of their feelings of exclusion were: they received negative responses about having LGBT parents; they were discouraged by school staff from being open about their parents or family; and LGBT families were not included in school activities.[9]

Obviously, for many children of LGBT parents, school is an unpleasant, if not outright dangerous and hostile experience. However, their needs have been have been marginalized by a focus on the school experiences of LGBT youth. In her book *Let's Get This Straight*, Tina Fakhrid-Deen interviewed the children of LGBT parents across the

United States. Not surprisingly, a prevailing topic was their school experiences. As she notes, "Although we receive less attention, children with gay parents often experience or witness anti-LGBTQ backlash and exclusion that is similar to that experienced by gay students."[10] Unfortunately, these students may delay or avoid seeking help from teachers or administrators for academic or social issues because they recognize that these concerns will reflect on their parents and family as a whole.[11] And these children may also not tell their parents of these same problems (including mistreatment) in order to protect them from a hostile school environment or to keep school officials oblivious to their family makeup.[12] Thus they doubly isolate themselves."

The School Experiences of LGBT Parents

Geographic of financial constraints (or both) mean that many LGBT parents have few options as to where their children attend school. Forty-six percent of LGBT parents who send their children to private, secular schools report that a primary reason for sending their children to a particular institution is its reputation for being welcoming.[13] But this choice it out of the reach of many LGBT parents—the average annual tuition at a private school is $8,549 but rises to $17,316 for a non-sectarian private school.[14] And even for those parents who have the resources to pay for a private school, not all schools are open to the children of LGBT families. In sum, the majority of LGBT parents (78 percent) send their children to public school.[15]

One of the earliest studies (1992) of gay and lesbian parents found that many did not disclose their sexuality and family configuration to schools due to an apparent or perceived lack of respect, tolerance, and welcoming. Additionally, many gay and lesbian parents were living in fear of being outed, resulting in negative consequences for both themselves their children. The study also recognized parents' concerns that remaining closeted might inadvertently send a negative message to their own children about the desirability of same-sex parents.[16] Though this study is now more than twenty years old—and in spite of Gay-Straight Alliances (GSAs); growing acceptance of LGBT families; national, state, and local efforts at tolerance; and antibullying programs—the experiences of LGBT parents two decades ago is still uncomfortably reminiscent of the struggles that today's parents confront.

On the positive side, *All Children Matter: How Legal and Social Inequalities Hurt LGBT Families*, a comprehensive 2011 overview of LGBT parents in the United States, cites research that finds that these parents are *more likely* than heterosexual parents to be involved in their children's schools—more likely to volunteer, to attend parent-teacher conferences, and to contact teachers about their children's academic performance or school experience.[17] The report, however, draws a sobering conclusion about the reason for this investment: it is yet another manifestation of the need to appear perfect in the community so as to nullify doubts as to LGBT parents' competence.[18]

Involved, Invisible, Ignored examined the experiences of LGBT parents with children attending kindergarten through twelfth grade. The majority of parents reported a relatively low incidence of negative experiences with school personnel. However, 26 percent reported that other parents at school had mistreated them and 21 percent described hearing negative comments about being LGBT from other students at their children's school.[19] One dramatic example cited was the experience of a lesbian mother who teaches in the same school her children attend:

> My main problem is with other parents. I keep my personal life private because I work at the school my children attend. As a teacher, I don't feel I have to announce anything, but other parents who have assumed that I'm a lesbian have made a point of spreading the word. There was also a teacher who thought it was her place to "out" me to the other teachers at a meeting that I was not at. I have had to file a police report on a parent for putting their hands on my son and screaming and calling me a "stupid lesbian bitch" in the office while my stepson's class was passing.[20]

Sometimes one parent receives the brunt of school-related opprobrium, and often this is the nonbiological parent. Consider this parent's observation: "The teacher's assistant almost always ignores my partner or is short with her, especially if she picks up my daughter without me . . . Also people always want to know who is the 'real' parent, meaning who gave birth to our girls."[21]

Like their children, lesbian and gay parents reported feeling excluded. One parent, for example, said, "For mother's day, my son's teacher did not allow him to make two items [one for each mother], only permitting my son to make one mother's day gift when clearly the teacher knows there are two mothers."[22] Another reported, "[We] just don't get invited to participate or volunteer at school functions or outings."[23] Overall, more than half of the parents surveyed reported some form of exclusion, and a quarter felt this exclusion as an overall feeling of neglect and invisibility. Additionally, a sizable number of parents also reported intrusive questioning about their family and even sex lives.

Sometimes the most difficult aspect for LGBT parents is watching their child suffer not only at the hands of other children but through the actions of adults in the school who are supposed to be supporting them. One mother wrote, "My daughter was bullied by a lunch lady who insisted that every child has a daddy. When I followed up with the teacher, principal, and assistant superintendent, they all conveyed to me that this was simply a 'misunderstanding' and a great deal of time and effort was spent to help me understand the lunch lady's perspective and 'background.'"[24] Another recalled, "My nine-year-old daughter received pro-Christian, antigay literature in her backpack from a classmate. The child's mother indicated to the child that the pamphlets were because my child had parents that were going to hell—but that the mother loved my child anyway."[25]

Finally, some parents recognized that their own children's discomfort about their family configuration prevented any meaningful intervention for school challenges. One parent reported, "My son is very concerned about his peers and what they will think of my relationship. Since he is in middle school and there is a lot of homophobia among his peers, I have agreed to let him be the one to tell people. As far as I know, he has only told one other person."[26] Another reported, "At the fifth-grade graduation, my child did not want me to attend, and would not state a specific reason, only to say that the other children gave her a hard time about me since I am not her birth mother."[27]

The Need for an LGBT-Friendly Curriculum

Student populations across the country are growing increasingly diverse. A common approach schools take is to minimize differences by treating each and every student the same; managing diversity means ignoring diversity. A more progressive approach, one that is fortunately on the rise, considers the multiple needs and perspectives of all students. Indications of this approach include cultural celebrations, bulletin board displays, and the hiring of staff from diverse backgrounds. However, many progressive educators believe that such measures are not enough. In the collection *Rethinking Multicultural Education*, Enid Lee, the renowned author of two books on multicultural education and the former supervisor of race/ethnic relations for the North York Board of Education in Toronto, writes: "First there is the surface stage in which people change a few expressions of culture in the school. They make welcome signs in several languages and have a variety of foods and festivals. My problem is not that they start there. My concern is that they often stop there . . . You don't have to fill your head with little details of about what other cultural groups eat and dance. You need to take a look at your culture, what your ideal of normal is, and realize it is quite limited and is in fact just reflecting a particular experience."[28]

Lee asks tough questions: Whose perspective is heard? Whose is ignored? In whose interest is it that we study what we study? Why is it that certain kinds of knowledge are hidden? The most advanced form of multicultural education doesn't seek merely to instill students with facts about different cultures but aims instead to examine the biases of the dominant culture and teach skills to challenge inequality and prejudice. According to Stuart Biegel, a member of the education and law faculty at UCLA and the author of *The Right to Be Out: Sexual Orientation and Gender Identity in America's Public Schools,* "Scholars have found overwhelmingly that an inclusive curriculum reflecting the existence of diverse communities in our pluralistic society benefits everyone and hurts no one."[29] In regard to the inclusion of gay, lesbian, and bisexual and transgender topics into the scholastic curriculum, he said, "A gay-inclusive curriculum not only helps create a welcoming and supportive environment for all students but has a particularly important benefit for gay and gender-nonconforming youth, the children of LGBT parents, and the friends and families of LGBT students in education settings."[30]

A common complaint and concern by LGBT parents and their children reported in the *Involved, Invisible, and Ignored* study was that their families were elided or excised from school curricula. Less than a third of students (27 percent) and parents (29 percent) reported that the school curriculum had included representations of LGBT people, history, or events in the past school year. When these topics were included, less than a quarter (21 percent) of all students in the survey reported positive representations of LGBT people, history or events.[31]

In December 2010, California state senator Mark Leno introduced the Fair, Accurate, Inclusive, and Respectful (FAIR) Education Act to prohibit discriminatory education and ensure that LGBT people are fairly and accurately included in instructional materials. The bill prohibited the State Board of Education from adopting instructional materials that discriminate on the basis of sexual orientation or gender identity. According to Leno, "Most textbooks don't include any historical information about the LGBT movement, which has great significance to both California and U.S. history. Our collective silence on this issue perpetuates negative stereotypes of LGBT people and leads to increased bullying of young people. We can't simultaneously tell youth that it's OK to be yourself and live an honest, open life when we aren't even teaching students about historical LGBT figures or the LGBT equal rights movement."[32] Despite the inevitable backlash, the bill was signed into law on July 14, 2011. Immediately, a coalition of antigay groups, including the National Organization for Marriage and the Family Research Council

(FRC), began collecting petitions ballot referendum to overturn the act. FRC's president, Tony Perkins, offered a summary of the arguments against FAIR, an act that "indoctrinates" youth with a curriculum that not only introduces students to transgender, bisexual, and homosexual identities but also sanctions them. First, students in California schools are already falling behind in core subjects (science, math, and reading) so they shouldn't be diverted from these areas to placate the "political agenda of a few." Second, the cost of new textbooks and classroom materials containing "this propaganda" is too onerous in the current financial climate. Third, teachers and school administrators will be forced to "violate their consciences by advocating for behavior they find morally objectionable." Finally, children will be "indoctrinated" by these educational materials.[33] In a PowerPoint presentation, FRC illustrates the deplorable impact of FAIR in one particular image in which parents are warned that students will now learn less about George Washington in order to learn about Chaz Bono.[34] In spite of (or possibly because of) this hyperventilating hyperbole, the required number of signatures necessary to force a referendum was not obtained.

Mombian founder Dana Rudolph has written about her efforts to find children's books about LGBT events and people: "The fact is, children's books about real LGBT people and LGBT civil-rights events are even scarcer than children's LGBT-inclusive fiction books. . . . Even if schools or teachers want to offer inclusive materials, there are none to be found." Rudolph found three books targeting elementary and middle school children.[35] Even if such resources did exist, according to Paul Boneberg, executive director of the GLBT Historical Society in San Francisco, "I'm not sure how we plug it into the curriculum at the grade school level, if at all."[36] Thus the California FAIR Act is indeed on the cutting edge of inclusiveness.

Of course, the efforts of the religious right and some social conservatives to preclude inclusive education have gone hand in hand with their efforts to make public schools more Christian. The religious right's constant attempts to "Christianize" (as that movement narrowly defines its faith) public schools also threaten the freedom to learn about many topics beyond LGBT-related issues. Battles over school curricula are occurring across the country, and they are not relegated to small communities. Consider the state of Texas. In 2011, governor Rick Perry appointed Barbara Cargill to serve as chair of the state school board. She described the debate over science education a "spiritual battle" in which she favors teaching the "strengths and weaknesses of evolution," including creationism.[37] In 2011, Oklahoma representative Sally Kern introduced HB 1551, the Scientific Education and Academic Freedom Act, which allows teachers to present creationist concepts without fear of losing their jobs.[38] Florida representative Stephen Wise sponsored SB 1854, which would amend Florida state law and require public schools to engage in "critical analysis" of evolution.[39] On the surface, these machinations may not sound overtly threatening to LGBT issues, but when one recalls that the creationists teach that homosexuality is a "genetic mistake" and a result of "original sin," we can be sure that schools adopting these policies wouldn't be welcoming to LGBT families.

Of course, creationism isn't the only focus of those attempting to "Christianize" education. In Arkansas, Kentucky, Mississippi, Virginia, and Missouri, bills have been introduced that would allow public schools to develop Bible-study courses, offer prayers in public schools, and/or display overtly religious symbols (typically the Ten Commandments) on school grounds. According to Citizens United, an organization dedicated to the separation of church and state, politicians across the country are attempting to "inject religion into public schools, foster unconstitutional forms of government-sponsored religion and obliterate strong protections that prevent state funding of religious institutions, including allowing taxes to fund schools that teach religious dogma."[40]

Censorship

In 2006, in the seemingly gay-friendly haven of Lower Merion, Pennsylvania, Steve Sokoll, a child psychiatrist raising two children with his partner, donated the book *And Tango Makes Three*—a children's book based on a true story about two male penguins raising a baby—to the school library. The school district was loud in its refusal of the book. "I found your gift to the classroom to be unacceptable," an official wrote in a letter to Sokoll. Sokoll argued his point, but the school district refused to acquiesce.[41]

In 1982 the US Supreme Court struck down a New York school district's attempt at book censorship. As Justice William Brennan wrote, "Local school boards may not remove books from school libraries simply because they dislike the ideas contained in those books and seek by their removal to 'prescribe what shall be orthodox in politics, nationalism, religion, or other matters of opinion.'"[42] Nevertheless, such efforts continue today. According to the American Library Association (ALA), approximately 85 percent of the challenges to library materials receive no media attention and remain unreported. Moreover, this statistic is limited to books and does not include challenges to magazines, newspapers, films, broadcasts, plays, performances, electronic publications, or exhibits. Sex, profanity, and racism remain the primary categories of objections.[43] Not surprisingly, books with positive LGBT characters are often a source of community ire. *And Tango Makes Three* is the most banned book in the last half decade; individuals and groups in at least fifteen states have challenged libraries over it, seeking to have the book labeled with a content warning, moved to a different section of the library, or removed from shelves altogether, according to the ALA's Office of Intellectual Freedom.[44]

Of the students who took part in the *Involved, Invisible, Ignored* study, only a little more than a quarter (29 percent) said that their school library contained materials that included LGBT-related topics.[45] Forty-five percent also said that they were able to use school computers to access websites about LGBT-related information.[46] Public schools use web-filtering software to block students' access to pornographic websites. This is in accordance with federal law; however, the software also blocks LGBT websites that are not sexually explicit, including the websites for LGBT rights organizations. At the same time, they allow access to anti-LGBT sites that condemn LGBT people or urge them to try to change their sexual orientation. In one example, in 2009, Andrew Emitt, a high school senior in Knoxville, Tennessee, used the computer in his school library to search for scholarship information for LGBT students. However, every website for an LGBT organization that came up in his search engine turned out to be blocked by his school district's web-filtering software. Upon further investigation, he found that organizations espousing antigay perspectives were accessible. "I wasn't looking for anything sexual or inappropriate," said Andrew. "I wasn't looking for games or chat rooms or dating sites. I was just looking for information about scholarships for LGBT students, and I couldn't get to it because of this software."[47]

The ACLU began its "Don't Filter Me" campaign in February 2011 by asking students to find out whether their schools were blocking web content that provides resources for LGBT students or expresses support for the equal treatment of LGBT people while allowing anti-LGBT viewpoints. By August 31, the ACLU had investigated and confirmed eighty-four reports of anti-LGBT-viewpoint discriminatory web filtering at public schools in twenty-four states.[48] According to Joshua Block, staff attorney with the ACLU LGBT project, "These filters are designed to discriminate and programmed specifically to target LGBT-related content that would not otherwise be blocked as sexually explicit or inappropriate. Public schools have a duty to provide students with viewpoint-neutral access to the Internet."[49] ACLU senior staff attorney Mary Catherine Roper added, "We aren't talking about sex websites—we're talking about websites that help high school students learn about themselves and about social issues. That's part of how schools prepare students for life."[50]

As a result of the "Don't Filter Me" campaign, many of the schools that were found to be filtering LGBT content have made changes to their software programs; others, though, have been less responsive, and the ACLU is in the process of pre-litigation negotiations.

Creating Safer Schools

In December 2008, the Milwaukee Board of Education approved the opening of the country's first gay-friendly middle school. The Alliance

School, serving sixth, seventh, and eighth graders, was the brainchild of Tina Owen, an English teacher and a lesbian raising five children with her partner. "I was hearing horrible stories about kids bullied and beat up and not coming back to school anymore," Owen said. "[Parents] want their kids in a safe place."[51] The Alliance School is not the first gay-friendly school in the United States; Harvey Milk High School in New York is the most renowned of these institutions. In 2008, Chicago attempted to create a similar school. The school, originally christened with the unwieldy moniker School for Social Justice Pride Campus, quickly attracted the attention of social conservatives, and changes occurred rapidly. The proposed school was renamed Solidarity High School. Since its critics had argued that LGBT teens aren't the only ones being bullied and that taxpayer dollars shouldn't be used to provide a one-sided education on this topic, the school expanded its mission to create a safe environment for all students who had experienced bullying and mistreatment in other schools. Eventually, the project was scuttled.

It should be noted that it isn't just social conservatives and the religious right who object to the creation of schools targeting sexual-minority youth; many allies and even LGBT individuals express their concerns. According to principal Chad Weiden of the failed Chicago effort, "We had the most resistance from within the LGBT community."[52] Ritch Savin-Williams, a professor at Cornell University who chairs the human development department, stated, "Being segregated doesn't help gay kids learn, it doesn't help straight kids learn, it doesn't help bullies learn. All it does is relieve the school and the teachers of responsibility."[53] Opponents dubbed the school "Homo High" and suggested that its creation gave other schools an impression that intolerance would be acceptable elsewhere. They also expressed concern that these students would not learn the skills to cope with an often homonegative world.

Regardless of the presence of the few gay-friendly schools, the overwhelming majority of communities do not offer schools for LGBT students or even describe their respective educational institutions as "gay-friendly." Many schools, though, have created gay-straight alliances (GSAs), school clubs that foster an environment of respect and acceptance. According to GLSEN, GSAs "improve school climate for LGBT students. When a GSA is present, LGBT students hear homophobic remarks less often, experience less harassment and assault, feel safer at school, skip school less often and have a greater sense of belonging."[54] Four thousand GSAs are registered with GLSEN.[55] Still, a study of the children of LGBT parents found only about a third (34 percent) said that their school had a GSA or other kind of student club that addressed LGBT student issues. Additionally, an intriguing 2011 study called into question the benefit of GSAs for schools demonstrating high levels of hostility and intolerance. It found that GSAs are most beneficial for schools *that already have low rates of LGBT victimization.*[56] According to the study's authors, "[T]his finding suggests that the creation of and membership in GSAs in schools cannot be accepted by schools as the only solution for creating safer school climates for LGBT youth."[57]

Some schools administrations and concerned parents also actively resist the presence of GSAs in their schools. But this is difficult to do without running afoul of the federal Equal Access Act, a 1984 law stipulating that if a public school allows any non-curriculum-based student club to meet during noninstructional time, it must allow them all. Ironically, the religious right originally promoted this act, since it opened the doors to the formation of Christian clubs on school grounds. Now some believe it has gone too far, particularly in regard to clubs supportive of sexual minorities. In one case, administrators at the Four Bluffs High School in Corpus Christi, Texas, decided to ban all student clubs rather than allow a GSA to meet. After the ACLU threatened legal intervention, school administrators capitulated and permitted the alliance to meet.[58]

The final component of the triumvirate to create safer schools for LGBT youth, along with gay-friendly schools and GSAs, is antibullying efforts. In October 2010, Secretary of Education Arne Duncan issued a guidance letter to schools and colleges reminding them that failure to address bullying could result in financial penalties from the federal government. "We're going to really challenge places that have their heads in the sand and aren't displaying the courage to move ahead in the right direction," said Duncan.[59] President Obama reiterated this, declaring, "We have an obligation to ensure that our schools are safe for all of our kids. Every single young person deserves the opportunity to learn and grow and achieve their potential, without having to worry about the constant threat of harassment."[60] The department is also conducting case studies in twenty-four school sites on the effectiveness and implementation of bullying policy.

At present, forty-five states have already passed laws addressing bullying or harassment in school, and ultimately it is state officials who determine whether new or revised legislation and policies should be introduced to update, improve, or add bullying-prevention provisions.[61] However, a November 2011 controversy regarding Michigan's belated attempt to pass anti-bullying legislation demonstrates the obstacles that can occur with even the most well-intentioned efforts to protect students. The bill, called Matt's Safe School Law (stemming from the 2002 bullying-related suicide of freshman Matthew Epling), had been unsuccessfully introduced into the Michigan legislation several times. But in the most recent effort, new wording was inserted that negated much of what had come earlier in the bill. The extra paragraph states that the bill "does not abridge the rights under the First Amendment . . . of a school employee, school volunteer, pupil or pupil's parent or guardian" and that it does not "prohibit a statement of a sincerely held religious belief or moral conviction of a of a school employee, school volunteer, pupil or pupil's parent or guardian."[62]

LGBT activists and advocates were quick to pounce. Nationally syndicated columnist D'Anne Witkowski wrote, "It's kind of hard to imagine why a legislative body would want to yank the fangs out of a measure initially designed to protect children. That is, until you consider that Michigan is one of the few states that doesn't have an anti-bullying law due, in large part, to anti-gay advocates who have fought against such a measure for years fearing that it would violate the religious freedom of anti-gay students. . . . Wouldn't this bill protect a bully telling a suspected gay classmate that homosexuals should be stoned to death. . . . And don't these statements create the kind of climate that so many LGBT students have found intolerable to the point of suicide?"[63] Matthew Epling's father was dismayed by the interpolation of a religious exception for bullying in school: "They kind of snuck in this extra paragraph, really kind of setting apart kids that feel their religious beliefs, their moral convictions, basically, can allow them to bully. . . . That one paragraph, though, negates most of the things we tried to put in."[64]

✦ ✦ ✦

The *Involved, Invisible, Ignored* study succinctly summarized the school experience of children of LGBT parents: "For many students with LGBT parents, school is not a very safe environment."[65] While several prominent organizations such as the Family Equality Council and GLSEN have formulated guidelines and recommendations for schools in regard to LGBT parents and their children, they are often not implemented. Currently, most of the efforts at creating safe, respectful, and inclusive schools—LGBT-friendly schools, GSAs, and anti-bullying legislation—target LGBT youth. Still, these efforts no doubt foster better school climates for the children of LGBT parents, even if their experiences and needs are not in the forefront of those promoting these changes. Fortunately, the last half decade has given a voice to these families, and they are bringing it to bear on this challenging aspect of LBGT family life.

6

Professional Services

The Presidential Citizens Medal is the second-highest civilian honor in the United States (outranked only by the Presidential Medal of Freedom) and is awarded by the president to citizens who have performed exemplary deeds or services for their country or fellow citizens. On October 20, 2011, President Obama granted Janice Langbehn this award for her efforts to ensure equality for all Americans.

In 2007, Langbehn, her partner Lisa Pond, and their three children were about to depart from Miami on a family cruise when Pond suddenly collapsed and was rushed to Jackson Memorial Hospital. She had had an aneurysm. Hospital personnel would not allow Janice or their children to see Lisa until nearly eight hours after their arrival, even though Lisa's sister was allowed to visit as soon as she arrived. The next day, Lisa died.[1]

The citation for Langbehn, read by a military aide, stated, "Janice Langbehn transformed her own profound loss into a resounding call for compassion and equality. When the woman she loved, Lisa Pond, suddenly suffered a brain aneurysm, Janice and her children were denied the right to stand beside her in her final moments. Determined to spare others from similar injustice, Janice spoke out and helped ensure that same-sex couples can support and comfort each other through some of life's toughest trials. The United States honors Janice Langbehn for advancing America's promise of equality for all."[2]

All LGBT parents will undoubtedly need to seek out medical care at some point for their children and themselves, and most of it will be for far less catastrophic events than Lisa Pond's case. Still, as the Human

Rights Campaign's 2011 *Healthcare Equality Index 2011* reported, LGBT people often decline to seek health care in times of need because they fear discrimination and poor treatment by health-care professionals.[3]

Are these concerns justified? In 2011 the Stanford School of Medicine's Lesbian, Gay, Bisexual and Transgender Medical Education Research Group surveyed 175 medical schools in the United States and Canada and found that 33.3 percent of respondents spent zero instructional hours on LGBT health and that, on average, these institutions offered five hours on LGBT issues.[4] Senior author Dr. Mitchell Lunn, an internal medicine resident at Brigham and Women's Hospital/Harvard Medical School said, "We heard from the deans that a lot of these important LGBT health topics are completely off the radar screens of many medical schools."[5]

Additionally, research on health issues in LGBT populations is marginal. According to Robert Garofalo, an associate professor of pediatrics at the Northwestern University Feinberg School of Medicine, who reviewed the state of knowledge of LGBT health in 2011, "No matter what we looked at, there was a paucity of research in the available literature."[6] Gaps included

- Most research relies on convenience samples, instead of large, random sample surveys
- Most of the research focuses on adults, not youth
- Most of the survey participants live in large cities (According to Garofalo, "We don't know what it's like to be LGBT and live in rural Illinois or the suburbs. There was no literature out there for us to pull from."[7])
- Most of the research on these populations has focused on lesbians and gay men and comparatively little on bisexual and transgender people

In 2010 Lambda Legal released a report detailing the health-care experiences of almost five thousand LGBT individuals and those living with HIV.[8] Almost 56 percent of lesbian, gay, or bisexual respondents had at experienced at least one of the following: being refused needed care; health-care professionals refusing to touch them or using excessive precautions; health-care professionals using harsh or abusive language; being blamed for their health status; or health-care professionals being physically rough or abusive.[9]

Ironically, the majority of respondents of this survey were more privileged than the LGBT population as a whole, with higher proportions holding advanced degrees, having higher household incomes, and having better health insurance coverage. For this reason, Lambda Legal acknowledges its report likely *understates* the barriers to health care experienced by all LGBT people. For example, in nearly every category, a higher proportion of respondents who are people of color and/or low-income reported experiencing discriminatory and substandard care.[10]

The Joint Commission, an independent, nonprofit organization that accredits and certifies more than nineteen thousand health-care organizations and programs in the United States, concluded that the "8.8 million lesbian, gay, and bisexual people now estimated to be living in the United States experience disparities not only in the prevalence of certain physical and mental health conditions but also in health care due to lack of awareness and insensitivity to their unique needs. These issues include the denial of visitation access, restrictions on medical decision making for LGBT family members, a distrust of the health care system and hesitation to disclose their sexual orientation or gender identity to medical professionals."[11]

Finally, LGBTs are twice as likely as the general population to be underinsured or completely lacking health insurance coverage. There are several reasons for this. First, they are more likely to lose or quit their jobs, to be employed in lower-wage jobs with no benefits, or to not be hired in the first place. Second, many workplaces do not provide spousal health insurance benefits for their employees involved in same-sex relationships. Finally, as a result of the current tax law structure, an employee with a same-sex partner must pay payroll taxes on the cash value of any domestic partner benefits, which increases the cost of insurance for these couples by an average of $1,100 per year, compared with married heterosexual workers.[12]

As summarized in the 2011 report *Changing the Game: What Health Care Reform Means for Lesbian, Gay, Bisexual, and Transgender Americans*, "[T]oo many lesbian, gay, bisexual and transgender people were destined to remain uninsured and unable to afford regular checkups and basic medical care. Too many in the LGBT community faced the prospect of continuing to go to bed at night worrying about paying their health care bills, and too many gay and transgender parents envisioned a future where they would continue to be unable to afford to take their children to the doctor."[13]

Recent Advances

The two years prior to the publication of this book were a period of momentous achievement in health care for LGBT individuals and their families. First, in April 2010, President Obama issued a memorandum calling on the Department of Health and Human Services to create regulations protecting the hospitalization visitation rights of all Americans, a directive that has vast implications for LGBTs. These new rules, which went into effect in January 2011, apply to hospitals participating in Medicaid and Medicare programs (the vast majority of hospitals) and ensure that all patients have their visitation rights respected. The regulations require hospitals to permit patients to designate visitors of their choosing and prohibit discrimination in visitation policies, including sexual orientation and gender identity. Medical facilities must allow equal access for same-sex couples and equal access for same-sex parents.

Second, the Joint Commission aligned its own polices with the new HHS requirements on July 1, 2011, with a goal of creating welcoming and supportive medical institutions for LGBT staff and patients. Among these policies:[14]

- Hospitals must prohibit discrimination based on sexual orientation and gender identity or expression, and this requirement applies regardless of local law.

- Hospitals should recognize same-sex partners as the patient's family, including recognizing same-sex marriages, even if these are not recognized by the law of the state in which the hospital is located.
- Hospitals should involve same-sex parents in their children's care, even those parents who lack legal custody.

Third, LGBT advocates were elated in 2011 when the Institute of Medicine released a 348-page report titled *The Health of Lesbian, Gay, Bisexual and Transgender People: Building a Foundation for Better Understanding.*[15] This report repeatedly reveals the current paucity of knowledge regarding LGBT health and the need for much more research. Bradley Jacklin, policy manager at the National Gay and Lesbian Task Force, stated, "This is historic. This is the first time the federal government has laid out a blueprint of the health challenges facing the LGBT community."[16]

Finally, the passage of the Affordable Care Act will allow LGBTs and their children access to the health insurance so many currently lack. This health-care reform law, passed in March 2010, expands access to health care for millions of people in America. In conversation with LGBT communities, Kathleen Sebelius, secretary of Health and Human Services, spelled out the specific benefits of the act for LGBTs and their families, including

- Outlawing the practice of rescinding policies because of technical mistakes and banning a lifetime coverage limit
- Ensuring free preventative care and immediately outlawing the practice of denying children policies because of pre-existing conditions
- Ensuring transparency in health-care coverage, including a new online tool for LGBTs to search for insurance companies that offer benefits for same-sex partners
- Investments in the health-care workforce
- Collection and integration of data on sexual orientation and gender identity in national health surveys[17]

(As this book goes to press, the Affordable Care Act has been found to be constitutional by the Supreme Court of the United States but continues to face political denunciation at the state and national levels.)

Mental Health Treatment

Health-care coverage is needed not only for medical problems but also for the treatment of mental health concerns. The LGBT community has consistently been found to have an elevated risk for substance use and mental health conditions such as depression, anxiety, eating disorders, and suicidal ideation, and many sufferers often struggle to pay for these services.[18]

According to the National Alliance on Mental Illness, 4 million children and adolescents in this country suffer from a serious mental disorder that causes significant functional impairments at home, at school, and with peers. Of children ages nine to seventeen, 21 percent have a diagnosable mental or addictive disorder that causes at least minimal impairment. Shockingly, in any given year, only 20 percent of children with mental disorders are identified and receive mental health services.[19] According to Mental Health America, estimates of the number of children who have mental disorders range from 7.7 million to 12.8 million.[20] The most common mental health concerns for young people are attention deficit hyperactivity disorder (ADHD), autism spectrum disorder, anxiety disorders, depression, bipolar disorder, learning disorders, conduct disorder, eating disorders, oppositional defiant disorder, post-traumatic stress disorder, risk-taking behavior, schizophrenia, and suicide.[21]

We have almost no information on the mental health needs of LGBT families. While there is no evidence that the children of LGBT parents have more mental health problems or more severe problems than youth raised by straight parents, there is also no evidence that these children have fewer problems. However, we barely have an understanding of the mental health needs of LGBT individuals in general, and the history of LGBT mental health treatment is fraught with discriminatory practices.

In 1973 the American Psychiatric Association (APA) finally removed homosexuality from its manual of mental health conditions. Until this historic moment, gay men and women had been considered mentally ill; the result was that the majority hid their status, voluntarily sought treatment, or were involuntarily institutionalized and received punishing "treatments" such as electroconvulsive therapy (ECT, also known as shock therapy). Following Stonewall, and in tandem with the protest movements sweeping the country in the late 1960s and early 1970s, more and more activist group were vocal in their opposition to the APA's classification of homosexuality as a disorder. Under intense scrutiny and continually barraged by contingents of gay and lesbian activists willing to engage in organized and confrontational public battles, the APA reevaluated previous studies of gay men and lesbians and acknowledged that they were weak and could certainly not be generalized to the majority of this population. In fact, it was found that most sexual minorities were satisfied with their orientation; for those seeking help, societal homophobia and heterosexism were the root causes of the issues. In 1975, the other APA—the American Psychological Association—came to the same conclusion. The two most respected mental health organizations in the world had agreed that homosexuality was not a disease within two years of each other. This is considered a milestone in the unfolding history of LGBT individuals.

Activists rejoiced, and critics went on the warpath. Even today, almost forty years later, social conservatives and antigay forces decry these decisions. NARTH—an organization that supports reparative therapy (treatment to "cure" gay men and lesbians of their homosexuality) and that has been condemned by accredited mental health institutions at every level—continues to claim that that research has yet to unequivocally prove that same-sex desire is not a pathology.[22] Reparative therapy became an issue of national concern in 2011 and 2012 when Michele Bachmann became a presidential candidate. Bachmann's husband engages in this treatment for men and women who attend his Christian counseling center.

The responses of other organizations are far less reserved than NARTH. For example, the Family Research Council (FRC) brochure *The Top Ten Myths About Homosexuality* states, "Homosexuals experience considerably higher levels of mental illness and substance abuse than heterosexuals" and that "no other group of comparable size in society experiences such intense and widespread pathology."[23] Furthermore, FRC discounts the role of societal homophobia and heterosexism in the mental health conditions of sexual minorities. FRC also positions itself as one of the staunchest and most vitriolic opponents of findings that biology and genetics play a role in the development of sexuality; its stance is, "No one is born gay."[24] (Readers should be aware that FRC, not surprisingly, is equally strident in its opposition to gay and lesbian families: "An overwhelming body of social science research shows that children do best when raised by their own biological mother and father who are committed to one another in a lifelong marriage."[25])

In 2008, thirteen national organizations (the American Academy of Pediatrics, American Association of School Administrators, American Counseling Association, American Federation of Teachers, American Psychological Association, American School Counselor Association, American School Health Association, Interfaith Alliance Foundation, National Association of School Psychologists, National Association of Secondary School Principals, National Association of Social Workers, National Education Association, and School Social Work Association of America) cooperated to create *Just the Facts About Sexual Orientation and You*, a document meant to dispel the seemingly never-ending misappropriation and outright deliberate distortion of psychological research regarding LGBTs promulgated by antigay groups such as FRC.[26] This document asserted that "the idea that homosexuality is a mental disorder or that the emergence of same-sex attraction and orientation among some adolescents is in any way abnormal or mentally unhealthy has no support among any mainstream health and mental health professional organizations."[27] The coalition also strongly criticized reparative therapy.

This is the juncture at which we find ourselves at present. Forty years of research findings that sexual minorities are just as emotionally stable as their heterosexual counterparts versus a small but tenacious, persistent, and well-funded collaboration of antigay and conservative organizations that often have direct access to legislatures across the country. And this divisive understanding of homosexuality eventually reaches into the very professional domains often needed by LGBT families.

Seeking Treatment

After months of seeing the same magazine titles in the admissions area of a large behavioral health hospital, a gay male staff member unobtrusively inserted a trendy, gay-themed magazine into the pile. This particular periodical was tailored for the fashion-conscious gay man and was no more overtly sexual than the female-oriented magazines that were regularly offered. Still, when a housekeeping member found it, she took it to the head of the admissions department, who tossed it into the trash, muttering that some patients "might be insulted."

In her interview with me, Danese recalled an experience where the inpatient substance treatment facility her daughter was about to enter was not necessarily LGBT-friendly:

> When filling out the forms with the intake person she asked about our daughter's father; when I told her she had same-sex parents, she seemed baffled and unsure what to do. She hesitatingly smiled and crossed off "name of father" from the application and wrote "name of second mother" instead. . . . Our daughter was allowed one phone call a day, and she told me that the structure of her family was never discussed. What infuriated me the most, though, was that during the first week of treatment a "family day" was held in order to introduce parents and siblings to the essentials of recovery, and the lecturer never once mentioned same-sex parents. She did mention divorced, widowed, and single parents in additional to the traditional two-parent model, but same-sex parents were left untouched.

Ample research underscores this lack of available or well-prepared mental health support. In 2011, almost 28 percent of the respondents to a Lambda Legal health-care survey reported that not enough mental health professionals are available to help them.[28] In a 2005 review of the training and education of therapists for clinical competence in working with same-sex-parented families, Jackie Coates and Richard Sullivan of the University of British Columbia found that "knowledge, skills and experience are prerequisites for competent practice and that these are not generally achieved with respect to sexual-minority families through the educational programs of the disciplines most commonly providing family counseling (psychology, medicine and social work). While the codes of ethics of these professions may express value convictions that oblige adherents to practice in such a way as to affirm human dignity in diversity, these convictions alone will not necessarily produce competent practice."[29]

And Leslie Calman, executive director of the Mautner Project, writes, "Well-meaning staff may think that by 'treating everyone alike' they are being equitable. But if treating everyone alike means assuming everyone is heterosexual, it renders LGBT people invisible and fearful of being stigmatized. . . . Too often, the failure to clearly signal that it is safe to be open results in a LGBT person's reluctance to communicate details of her life that her provider ought to know."[30]

Some states may even be moving in the opposite direction of inclusive treatment. In May 2011, Arizona enacted a law allowing students in social work and counseling programs to discriminate. Students can now disregard the ethics of national accreditation boards and also avoid repercussions from their respective colleges and universities for refusing to work with clients whose behaviors they deem as contrary to their religious beliefs.[31] Thus a social work student performing an internship could refuse to work with a sexual minority if her religious beliefs find his or her behaviors to be immoral.

Religious right groups applaud this measure, and have come to the defense of Julea Ward on this issue. Ward was in an Eastern Michigan

University counseling program but was dismissed in March 2009 after she refused, as part of her training, to counsel a gay client. She told school administrators that she could not "affirm any behavior that goes against what the Bible says."[32] During a school hearing on her case, she stated she would not abide by school standards when they contraindicated her religious beliefs. Ward sued, stating that her religious liberty and free speech rites had been violated. She received the backing of the Alliance Defense Fund (ADF), whose website describes it as "a network of more than 2,000 allied attorneys nationwide [that] directly litigates carefully chosen, strategic cases to preserve and reclaim your God-given, constitutionally protected religious freedom, the sanctity of life, marriage, and the family."[33] Other religious right groups massed to support Ward and ADF, including the Justice and Freedom Fund, the Becket Fund for Religious Liberty, the American Center for Law and Justice, and the Foundation for Moral Law. Ward's proponents believe that the case will eventually reach the US Supreme Court.

According to David Kaplan, chief professional officer of the American Counseling Organization, the organization that accredits EMU, "We train students to understand that the client is more important than they are. Just because someone has different values, doesn't mean we can't counsel them. We don't have to agree with them, but we must accept them for who they are."[34]

Affirmations, a Detroit community center for sexual minorities, signed a friend-of-the-court brief in the case of Ward. Kathleen LaTosch, chief administrative officer of Affirmations, knows through her daily encounters just how important the relationship between counselor and client is when LGBT people seek mental health treatment: "There was a time a year ago when we were short of counselors. We couldn't take clients into our program for about six weeks, so we started to offer suggestions from our referral list. But our clients didn't want to go anywhere but here. They were willing to be on a waitlist thirty to forty people deep in order to come here. When you're in counseling, you talk about some really personal, sensitive issues. It's a very vulnerable place, and you can't afford to bring negativity into that."[35]

Affirmative Treatment Facilities

LGBT families who have access to treatment facilities specifically catering to sexual minorities are likely to receive respectful treatment. But such access is limited for most families. Instead, they have limited options—sometimes only a single provider that may even not even be near their own home. These families may know nothing about the staff with whom they will interact or even the treatment philosophies that exist there. Some providers hold to the belief that LGBT individuals are incapable of being good parents (or at least good-enough parents). Some hold to the recruitment myth that these parents are conscripting youth into an "alternative lifestyle." The most common challenge is professionals who focus on parents' sexuality as the underlying cause for any and all issues occurring in the family—even though it is unheard of to encounter clinicians who immediately assume that children are having problems because they are being raised by straight parents. Families are likely to encounter heterosexism and veiled homonegativity from staff and even other clients.

In *A Provider's Introduction to Substance Abuse Treatment for Lesbian, Gay, Bisexual, and Transgender Individuals,* the Center for Substance Abuse Treatment lists specific practices that indicate whether treatment providers have proficiency in treating sexual minorities.[36] From my own experience, I find that the following questions from the guide are most telling about any type of treatment facility when contemplating a specific treatment provider:

- Are *all* staff mandated to participate in trainings relating to sexual minorities?
- Do the forms, brochures, and educational materials *assume* heterosexuality as the norm?
- Does the facility promote and advertise its LGBT services?

- Does the facility's referral and resource list offer options relevant to LGBTs?
- Does the facility make family services available for same-sex partners and families of choice during treatment?
- Do education sessions and lectures include LGBT issues?
- Does the facility employ openly LGBT individuals as staff members?
- What are the guidelines for clients regarding homophobic behavior so that LGBT individuals are safe? How are these guidelines enforced?
- Does the facility provide education for heterosexual clients about language and behaviors that show bias toward LGBT people?
- How does the facility investigate complaints of discriminatory practices reported by LGBT clients and family members?

Joe Kort, one of the country's leading experts on gay-affirmative mental health treatment, notes that such treatment is not a specific modality but rather a way of helping sexual minorities move from shame to pride and undoing the damage of a "homophobic, homo-ignorant society, and heterosexist therapy."[37] Gay-affirmative treatment is an approach underlying the other therapeutic skills and interventions that are the stock and trade of mental health professionals.

According to Kort, there are three principles underlying affirmative treatment:

1. *Understanding and combating heterosexism:* The American Psychological Association issued a series of sixteen guidelines for working with sexual minorities. In addition to acknowledging that homosexuality and bisexuality are not indicative of mental illness, practitioners are called "to understand the ways in which social stigmatization (i.e., prejudice, discrimination, and violence) poses risks to the mental health and well-being of lesbian, gay, and bisexual clients."[38] Additionally, the Substance Abuse and Mental Health Services Administration recommends

that helping professionals assist their clients in healing from the negative effects of homophobia and heterosexism.

2. *Understanding heterosexual privilege:* Mental health professionals are reminded that heterosexuals have a gamut of taken-for-granted freedoms that are granted automatically that are not necessarily accessible for LGBT individuals and their families. Assuming LGBT families have the same freedoms as a straight family is a blunder on the part of clinician.

3. *Acknowledging one's own homophobia and homonegativity:* The American Psychological Association recommends that "psychologists are encouraged to recognize how their attitudes and knowledge about lesbian, gay, and bisexual issues may be relevant to assessment and treatment and seek consultation or make appropriate referrals when indicated."[39]

In sum, an gay-affirmative treatment provider—whether working in a clinic-based setting or out of his or her own office —is an individual who recognizes the societal and community challenges confronting LGBT individuals and their families, who has invested energy in analyzing his or her own preconceptions and emotions about sexual minorities, and who understands that most of the mental health concerns they present with are not caused by their sexuality but rather the impact of heterosexism and homonegativity on these men and women and the children they are raising.

Accessing Care

The Human Rights Campaign's annual *Healthcare Equality Index* offers readers a snapshot of progress (and lack of) made in treatment centers across the United States.[40] A LGBT parent can access information on 375 facilities in twenty-nine states and the District of Columbia. For example, a lesbian mother living in Philadelphia now has access to the following information on the Children's Hospital of Philadelphia, one of the leading pediatric health-care providers in the region:

- Patient nondiscrimination policies
- Visitation policies
- Cultural competency training and client services
- Employment policies and benefits

This is a great start; unfortunately, the report offers no guidance for LGBT families living in twenty-one states. Furthermore, only several facilities from each state responded to the survey. For example, in Pennsylvania, only two hospitals were willing to describe their efforts, and both are located in Philadelphia. There is no information regarding other health-care facilities in the state. While the number of respondents to HRC's health-care survey increase each year, a full accounting of facilities across the country in regard to basics such as discrimination policies, visitation policies, staff training, and employment policies and benefits will not be available in the near future.

What, then, are the options for LGBT families who have no access to the treatment facilities measured by the HRC survey or who live in urban areas without recognized specialized treatment providers? In particular, what are the options for families needing medical treatment living in less-than-welcoming communities? Lambda Legal's 2011 survey found that over half of LGBT respondents indicated that overall community fear or dislike of people like them is a barrier to care.[41]

Know the Law

Health-care laws vary widely from state to state. For example, the laws of my home state of Pennsylvania do not specifically provide for a partner to make decisions on behalf of an incapacitated same-sex partner. Contact must be attempted with *at least five individuals* before a partner would have authority. In contrast, the neighboring state of New Jersey has ruled that a civil union partner has the same rights and responsibilities as a spouse with regard to laws relating to emergency and nonemergency medical care and treatment, hospital visitation and notification, and any rights guaranteed to a hospital patient. The Human Rights

Campaign is an ideal place to initiate a search on the respective health-care laws for each state and their relevance for LGBTs.

There are several prevailing recommendations in regard to medical treatment that LGBT individuals and families should consider. The first urges that LGBTs create *advance health-care directives*—documents that spell out what measures a person wants taken when he or she is no longer capable of communicating choices regarding prolonging life and other medical care issues. Unfortunately, surveys over the past decade indicate that only 20 to 30 percent of Americans have formulated advance directives, and people of color and low-income individuals are less likely to have created them than whites.[42]

Since most medical decision-making law is not inclusive of LGBT families, it is especially important that LGBT families complete directives to ensure their ability to make medical decisions for incapacitated partners. Even if an LGBT individual has created an advance directive, there may be some situations in which health-care providers need additional information in order to decide what action should be taken. A durable power of attorney for health care (also sometimes called a *health-care proxy*) empowers someone to make medical decisions for another person if that person becomes unable to make these decisions for him- or herself. A few states have created advance directive registries. In these states, an adult can register his or her desires regarding end-of-life treatment and name a health-care proxy. This information in kept in an Internet database accessible by health-care agencies. Each state has its own protocol for validating health-care proxies, and LGBT parents are strongly advised to secure this information.

LGBTs are also advised to complete a *visitation authorization*, a document allowing a person to designate who will be able to visit him or her in the hospital if that person is no longer able to communicate. The presidential memorandum of April 15, 2010, summed up the plight succinctly: "Every day, all across America, patients are denied the kindnesses and caring of a loved one at their sides—whether in a sudden medical emergency or a prolonged hospital stay. . . . [U]niquely affected are gay and lesbian Americans who are often barred from the bedsides of the partners with whom they may have spent decades of their lives—unable to be there for the person they love, and unable to act as a legal surrogate if their partner is incapacitated."[43] This memorandum, sent by President Obama to the secretary of Health and Human Services, called for new guidelines regarding hospitals' compliance with existing regulations to guarantee that all patients' advance health-care directives are respected and that hospitals participating in Medicare and Medicaid programs cannot deny visitation privileges on the basis of race, color, national origin, religion, sex, sexual orientation, gender identity, or disability. These regulations went into effect in 2011.

Finally, for LGBT parents, a *consent for treatment* allows a partner to consent to emergency medical treatment for a child if a biological parent is not available. The National Center for Lesbian Rights suggests that even if both partners are recognized as legal parents, it is advisable to execute this document in case they are traveling in a state that refuses to recognize their relationship or parental status.[44]

✦ ✦ ✦

New regulations and guidelines, along with the growing acceptance of LGBT individuals and their families, are certain to lead to progress in their health care. However, this is a process. Some organizations will be more successful sooner than others.

When more than 50 percent of LGBTs report mistreatment by medical and mental-health-care providers, it is easy to understand their anxiety and even dread regarding accessing these services. In fact, many of the individuals I spoke to took a "guilty until proven innocent" approach; providers were assumed to be less than welcoming until they evinced proof to the contrary. Maris told me that her neighbor—a true straight ally if there ever was one—recommended her own children's pediatrician as the ideal doctor to work with her family. Maris, however, experienced unexpected blatant hostility from this small practice and did not at all feel welcome, respected, or even safe. Maris's neighbor was shocked at this report and indignantly contacted the provider, "gave him hell," and, from that point on, refused to work with him any longer.

If all LGBT families had neighbors like Maris's, their community experiences would surely be less turbulent. Unfortunately, they do not. Some families lie about their status, particularly designating one person to the "official" parent to shuttle a child to routine medical appointments while the identity of the other is elided or fabricated. Others carefully scrutinize the available options and select providers who are known to be LGBT affirmative even if the distance is far greater than closer local services. Many simply hope that no critical incident necessitates health-care proxies and visitation authorizations that might jeopardize their "secret."

Lambda Legal urges families to fight back when discrimination occurs by contacting Lambda Legal, other legal and advocacy organizations, or a local attorney. But for low-income families and those living in the closet in their local communities, these options are not realistic, at least at the present stage in the progress of LGBT rights. It is thus recommended that families create active support systems, including straight allies, who can and will fight on their behalf.

Beginning in 2010, the expectations and guidelines for medical providers and mental health regarding LGBTs have evolved at an astounding rate, with some advocates claiming the changes occurring during the two years following equal the importance of the American Psychiatric Association's 1973 decision to remove homosexuality from its manual of mental illnesses. Still, setbacks can occur. For example, Emilia Lombardi, a professor at the University of Pittsburgh, expressed concern that the *Health of Lesbian, Gay, Bisexual and Transgender People* report could have a similar fate to earlier efforts, such as the 2001 US Department of Health and Human Services' *Strategic Plan on Addressing Health Disparities Related to Sexual Orientation*, a document commissioned during the Clinton administration but disregarded by

George W. Bush and his cabinet. According to Lombardi, "There are people in politics who don't have a good view of science overall."[45] Bradley Jacklin of the National Gay and Lesbian Task Force agrees: "Elections do matter. There's a risk of this becoming a doorstop if administrations change."[46] All of us—LGBTs and allies—must continue to advocate for continued improvements in laws and policies and fight efforts to roll back these gains.

7

Recreation and Leisure

I'm walking with Meredith through the sixty-one-acre theme park Silver Dollar City, located in Branson, Missouri. Her two children were set free to wander more than an hour ago, and they are expected to meet us for lunch at 1:30 at Aunt Polly's, one of the restaurants in the park, famous for its "southern-style fried catfish and ham and beans." The crowd is sparse, and I see more seniors than children.

"I'm sure this place is jammed during the summer; the rest of Branson is," Meredith tells me. Though she and her children relocated to Branson more than a decade ago, this is the first time she has been to the amusement park. "Of course, I know about the Silver Dollar City. If you live in—or anywhere near—Branson, you can't help but know of it. The traffic itself to and from the park is one of the biggest nightmares of living here."

As we wander through the park, she describes her life: "I don't live paycheck to paycheck; that would be a relief for me. Our paychecks are used to pay bills that are two months behind. Between Rose and myself, we have less than a thousand dollars saved. Rose needed a root canal earlier in the year, but she asked instead to have the tooth removed altogether. It was cheaper. We don't have dental insurance, and the little we do have saved is there for emergencies." Both mothers work in the hospitality industry; Meredith cleans hotel rooms and is occasionally responsible for setting up the hotel's complimentary breakfasts. Rose works the register at a chain store. Both receive unemployment for several months when the tourist season comes to its inevitable conclusion.

Families pass us along the often-steep hills of the park, and many parents are holding hands. Some are extended families with the children sandwiched between parents and grandparents. Often, we see whole families engaged in a prayer before they settle in at one of the park's restaurants. This isn't surprising, since the park is located directly in the Bible Belt and even its website announces upcoming Christian events such as the "Southern Gospel Picnic," "Young Christians' Weekend," and "Church of Christ Weekend," all offering "messages to feed the soul and awesome worship services."[1]

Meredith stares wistfully at one of the families passing. "I would love to come here with Rose and the kids and be as relaxed as these families are, but I don't foresee this happening. I don't see Rose and [me] holding hands in Silver Dollar City."

"What would happen?" I ask.

She contemplates before answering: "Nothing most likely. People might stare, and they might laugh. But I doubt anybody would say anything to our faces. Nobody would kick us out of the park. But are we welcome? I mean, really welcome?"

Fred asked the same question of Knoebels Amusement Park in Elysburg, Pennsylvania. I arranged to meet Fred, a single gay dad, for the afternoon, and he brought along his six-year-old daughter. Unlike Meredith, Fred was not only willing but eager to get on as many attractions as possible; for two of them, I waited with his daughter, who wasn't yet tall enough to participate. Unlike Silver Dollar City, which I visited in off-season, Knoebels was overflowing with patrons; lines for the amusements were often long and snaking.

"I've been here before—actually, many times; I even came here as a child when my family lived in New Jersey," Fred told me over lunch. "There's no admission charge, so it's a lot cheaper in the long run than some of the other parks in the state."

I told him about my afternoon at Silver Dollar City with Meredith, and he acknowledged her concern:

I started coming to this park before a lot of the rides you see right now were even built. It's part of my history. I never had the opportunity to go to Disney, and that's one of my dreams for Crystal [his daughter], but I don't have the resources right now. But would I come here—to a park I've known since childhood and that I have lots of fond memories of—would I come here as an openly gay family? I don't know. I see lots of teens wandering this park without parent supervision . . . something could happen—not necessarily violence, but some type of harassment or mocking. I could foresee an planned day at the park quickly devolving into a shameful experience for all of us.

All families have access to leisure and recreation activities, although some have more limited options than others. Meredith and Fred described some of the sports teams, camps, and civic associations existing in their communities in addition to the large amusement parks we had visited. Still, in spite of the availability of these options, LGBT families may need to be cautious in partaking of these opportunities and circumspect in how they behave in these settings. My conversations with parents across the country regarding youth development, leisure, and recreation opportunities continually led to two concerns: safety and shame. Regardless of the type of leisure and recreation facilities, the openness of these programs to LGBT parents and their children cannot be assumed.

James, for example, a gay father who has joint custody of his two sons with his ex-wife, told me of his first visit to his eleven-year-old son's soccer practice:

I wasn't out at that point, except to a few friends. Nobody warned me what go expect. From the moment we arrived at the field I was surrounded by the words "fag," "faggot," and "queer." Occasionally, an expletive would precede them. The kids used the words. Parents used the words. Even the coaches used the words. I couldn't believe it. My son and I had a long talk that next weekend about the power of words, and my personal dislike of these words. I certainly didn't want to hear him saying them. A few years later, I met a lesbian couple whose son was in the same league, but for a younger age group. I asked them how they handled it. They at first tried to dissuade their son from participating in the sport. When this didn't work, they reluctantly allowed him to sign up. It was soon apparent that he didn't want his teammates to know of his family's relationship status. They became his mother and his aunt.

Youth Development Programs

Over the last decade, many programs catering to youth (and their families) have begun to characterize themselves as youth development programs. Traditionally, we may think of these as leisure activities, but all play a role in youth development. As an example, the summer camp industry has implemented a national campaign promoting a new image of camps: they are no longer merely outdoor settings where children have fun but instead conduits for youth development. As summarized by the American Camp Association, "Camp is both a laboratory and a catalyst for child development. By studying campers' experiences and camp's impact on the lives of young people, ACA provides parents with the knowledge to make good decisions, to thoughtfully guide their children, and to offer opportunities for powerful lessons in community, character building, skill development, and healthy living. Camp is a powerful, positive force!"[2] And 4-H programs, often misidentified as agricultural programs, exist throughout the United States. On its website, 4-H describes itself as "the nation's largest youth development organization. . . . Using research-based programming around positive youth development, 4-H youth get the hands-on real world experience they need to become leaders."[3]

Even smaller organizations common in most communities, such as day camps, museums, and zoos, no longer view their programs as merely leisure and recreation activities that keep children entertained but now promote their youth development aspects. But these programs aren't necessarily successful for children of LGBT parents. Having been the residential director of Mountain Meadow Summer Camp, the first camp for children of same-sex parents, I heard many stories from parents about why they elected to send their children to our facility rather than a more convenient local camp. For example, Micah and Jeff located my camp after pulling their child from another. According to Micah:

> We were completely up-front with the camp director about our family, and she assured us that her staff was proficient and experienced in working with all children, regardless of their backgrounds. After our daughter revealed in a cabin meeting prior to bedtime that her parents were two men, all hell broke loose. Her peers ignored her or taunted her. Staff seemed unable to control this behavior, and their interventions only made the camper's taunting more furtive. Our daughter was miserable. When we finally picked her up after a week of this torture, I asked her counselor what training they had received regarding gay families. The answer—nothing. In their seven days of training to camp the topic had never been introduced.

Unfortunately, most youth development organizations have only recently caught on that LGBT families exist and use their services. Concerted efforts at inclusiveness for LGBT individuals and their families are still in their infancy. Dan Woog, one of the country's authorities on sports and LGBT issues and a vociferous supporter of LGBT youth, told me that in his many years of experience he found the people who manage and staff youth programs tend to be well-intentioned individuals who truly look out for the welfare of participants. The reason children of LGBT parents aren't a priority is simply that nobody has alerted these staff to their presence. He predicts that as their presence is increasingly recognized, youth programs will make an effort to create safe and welcoming environments.[4] Still, at present, many LGBT families cannot or will not come forward to demand better and more inclusive services; to do so would jeopardize their status and even safety in their communities.

One solution of course is to eschew local options. LGBT parents instead opt for the growing number of summer camps for children of

LGBT parents, the annual Family Pride Week in Provincetown, Massachusetts, and the small number of family vacation cruises and events such as those offered by R Family Vacations, a business started by Rosie and Kelli O'Donnell. (Though R Family activities have been hampered by antigay hostility. The first R Family cruise that arrived in Nassau, Bahamas, was met by protestors. According to the *New York Times*, "Their loud taunts caused some children on the ship to cry and induced Rosie O'Donnell to remain on deck—rather than enter into what was certain to be a televised shouting match."[5] In 2007, R Family canceled a planned stop in Bermuda after a religious group said to represent eighty Bermudian churches announced its opposition.[6]) And of course some traditional family destinations have become more LGBT friendly; the Disney Resorts stand as an exemplar.

But for families for whom such options are not feasible or realistic, the local community remains the primary provider of youth and family activities. Thus LGBT parents often keep their children out of youth programs or are less than forthcoming about their family's composition. This is unfortunate, because research unequivocally finds that a quality youth program is a conduit to successful adulthood.

Youth Programs as Conduits to Successful Adulthood

The goal of parenting is to guide one's children into successful adulthood. The term "successful adults" is of course open to interpretation. One set of parents may believe that raising their children to have a lifelong relationship with a higher power is a marker of success. Another set may believe success will be measured by their children's financial status. And a third may believe that a child who excels in one particular field is the ultimate indicator of success. None of these is exclusive of the others. However, in spite of these individualized and sometimes competing definitions, researchers have established an encompassing definition of "success" to which parents should be guiding their children. The *five Cs* model is commonly used, and it promotes ideals all children should develop:[7]

1. *Competence:* A positive view of one's actions in specific areas, including social, academic, cognitive, health, and vocational
2. *Confidence:* An internal sense of overall positive self-worth and self-efficacy
3. *Connection:* Positive bonds with people and institutions that are reflected in exchanges between the individual and his or her peers, family, school, and community in which both parties contribute to the relationship
4. *Character:* Respect for societal and cultural norms, possession of standards for correct behaviors, a sense of right and wrong (morality), and integrity
5. *Caring/compassion:* A sense of sympathy and empathy for others

A sixth "C" is also considered of increasing importance, though it has not yet been officially interpolated into the model: *Contribution* to family, community, society, and the planet.

The five Cs (or six Cs) model is an encompassing and thorough blueprint for successful adulthood; few would argue that adults achieving these goals are not successful. It is not surprising, therefore, that the majority of youth programs in the country use the five Cs model as a guide in their program development.

Three characteristics have been found to be essential for a quality youth program that supports the growth of the five Cs: a safe environment, supportive relationships, and opportunities to belong.[8] Yet these are the three characteristics that LGBT families find lacking in available programs in their local communities.

Safe Environment

One of the most important characteristics associated with successful youth programs is a safe environment; if children don't feel safe, their potential to enjoy the program let alone develop the five Cs is doubtful. Yet, in these programs, the children of LGBT parents may be excluded by their peers, talked about behind their back, and be coerced to keep their status a secret by well-intentioned staff members. Tragically, some youth become the victims of bullying and physical assault. Though children of LGBT parents report less physical harassment in comparison with verbal taunting and mistreatment, the number of youth subjected to physical mistreatment is by no means insignificant. One study found that about a tenth of students had been physically harassed or assaulted in the prior year because they had LGBT parents, because of their actual or perceived sexual orientation, or because of their gender or gender expression.[9] Other forms of victimization include being the target of mean rumors or lies, being sexually harassed, or having their property stolen or deliberately damaged. Keep in mind that a child may experience several forms of ongoing victimization and that this abuse doesn't occur just at the hands of other youth. Program leaders and other parents may also inflict harm.

Supportive Relationships

In 2010, Jon Langbert of Dallas, a Cub Scout leader and the gay father of a nine-year-old Cub Scout, was forced out of his leadership role due to his sexual orientation. The Boy Scouts of America has a longstanding and contentious policy of excluding gay men and atheists from leadership roles. According to Deron Smith, Boy Scouts of America's director of public relations, "We focus on our mission, and our mission is to take young people and prepare them for an exceptional adulthood. That's it. That's why our policy is the way it is. Our volunteer leadership has elected to keep that policy in place. . . . The policy, as it is written, is that the Boy Scouts does not accept for membership avowed homosexuals." Smith said Langbert was welcome to continue volunteering his time, though not as a leader. He also added that the issue would not have arisen had Langbert kept his sexual orientation private, since prospective leaders are not asked whether they are gay.[10]

According to Langbert, "Everything was running along smoothly until some of the dads complained. . . . It made me feel terrible to think about the devastating effect it would have on my son, to see his father stripped of his leadership role."[11]

Children and youth need supportive adult relationships, and so do their parents. But Jon Langbert's case shows, supportive relationships may be denied to LGBT families. Several parents I spoke to mentioned that programs staff were aloof, distant, and cold when they dropped off and picked up their children; other parents, they noted, were received warmly or at least cordially. "I don't believe that the day camp staff and director treat my child any differently that the children of straight parents, *but they treat me differently,*" reported Anne. "If they mistreated my kids or preached to them I would pull them out the program in a second. The problem though is that we don't have a lot of options."

The previous chapters stressed the importance of LGBT parents building a support system for themselves, one that ideally includes other same-sex parents and straight allies. The need for a support system is even more critical for the children of these families. Studies find that a combination of parental support, access to children of other same-sex parents, and straight allies offers the best outcomes for these youth. As this book has pointed out, however, this combination may not be feasible for LGBT-parented families, so some youth and their parents will have to piece together the best alternatives they can.

Marty, for example, knows of no other youth in his neighborhood or school who have two mothers. His older brother graduated from the same high school and never once disclosed the role of two mothers in his life; his parents are likewise reluctant to share their history other than with a few very close friends. Marty notes: "My moms coached me from a very young age to be less than honest regarding our family, and now that I'm older, I understand why. Our community is insular and fairly intolerant . . . [but then] I heard about COLAGE and made contact with people all over the country, so I created my own support network . . . though all of it is online. A gay-straight alliance also opened in our high school last year, and I joined."

Marty is creating his own support system of LGBTs and straight allies. His mother Jerri noticeably bristled when we discussed the importance of allies: "I read a story about lesbian mothers and their children at the annual White House Easter egg hunt. Donna and I would love to be able to so open and grace the pages of the national newspapers. But we live in a state where we can lose our jobs if our sexual identity was discovered. We could even lose our apartment. . . . Getting allies sounds easy, but try to find allies in this town who will guard your privacy. Right now, it is impossible."

Donna, Jerri's partner, is less despairing in her description of their hometown life, but she is equally pessimistic about finding an open "support system." She recounted: "I attend NA meetings, and I have many people who are supportive of [my] continued sobriety. But even these folks don't know about my sexual orientation. I gotta keep that a secret."

Mark Snyder of COLAGE reports that he has encountered too many youth who have spent their lifetimes hiding their families' secret.[12] They may have participated in sports, clubs, and other recreational activities throughout their youth but never once disclosed their family composition. This secrecy may have been the result of a parental directive or observing the negativity of peers and staff in these programs regarding LGBTs; often it is the result of both. COLAGE meetings—typically closed to adults—may be the only safe place where these youth can relax their otherwise perpetual vigilance

As the children of same-sex-parented families mature, they may actively seek out their own allies and support, as Marty did. They'll find information online or join a GSA or some other type of club in their school or community. As stated earlier in this book, the battles between children who are ready to disclose their identity and parents who are not remain a truly understudied phenomenon. Tracy, for example, states that reading Abigail Garner's *Families Like Mine* made such an impression that she was ready to "come out of the closet" in regard to her family.[13] Her mothers, however, were not, and this disagreement escalated into the worse fights than she ever could recall occurring between herself and her parents.

Younger children are much more reliant on parents to surround them with a nurturing support system. Even if there are no other known LGBT families around, parents should surround their children with individuals who fight against intolerance and hatred and who understand the travails that still come from being a minority group. These individuals treat all people with respect and dignity.

Belonging

The final requirement for a successful youth program is that it offers participants a sense of belonging and acceptance.

Families Like Mine gave a voice to the experiences of so many children of LGBT parents: they live in two worlds, the majority-straight world and the sexual-minority world. Of course, living within two cultures has its stressors, and navigating them does not necessarily come naturally or easily. In a seminal article on the topic, Teresa LaFromboise of the University of Wisconsin and her colleagues defined bicultural efficacy as the "belief, or confidence, that one can live effectively, and in a satisfying manner, within two groups without compromising one's sense of cultural identity."[14] It is imperative that children of sexual minorities develop this efficacy because they are indeed straddling two different worlds. Indeed, some youth are living in more than two distinct worlds. Consider, for example, African American children adopted by white LGBT parents. They have three overlapping worlds to circumnavigate.

While it is inarguable that the children of sexual minorities will learn about straight culture through their interactions with the majority population and exposure to media, we should not take it for granted that they will learn the history of the challenges, struggles, successes, and setbacks of lesbians and gay men. In the 2009 *National School Climate Survey*, almost 90 percent of LGBT students reported they had not been taught anything about the history of LGBT people.[15] In a 2008 study, less than a third of both students and parents reported that their school's curriculum had included representations of LGBT people, history, or events in the past school year.[16]

The Call for Inclusiveness

According to the Commission for Accreditation of Park and Recreation Agencies (CAPRA), "Every park and recreation agency, whatever its focus or field of operation, is rightfully concerned with the efficiency and effectiveness of its operations. With the importance of park and recreation programs and services to the quality of life, each agency has an essential role in the lives of the people it serves."[17] The Commission created 144 standards demonstrating commitment to its employees, volunteers, patrons, and community. One standard is outreach to underserved people: "Parks and recreation programs and services shall be available to all residents regardless of income, cultural background, geographic location, age, or ability level. To encourage participation in parks and recreation programs and services, agencies shall identify and address barriers that may limit access by special populations in the community."[18]

LGBT families are indeed an underserved population when it comes to local recreation, youth development, and leisure venues. LGBT parents and allies must guide and navigate their children through the myriad of formal and informal challenges that exist in community programs in spite of recommendations for inclusiveness and outreach such as CAPRA's. As an example, in 2011, GLSEN introduced its Sports Project with a mission "to assist K–12 schools in creating and maintaining an athletic and physical education climate that is based on the core principles of respect, safety and equal access for all, regardless of sexual orientation or gender identity/expression" and further advances its mission to "create a world in which every child learns to accept and respect all people, regardless of sexual orientation or gender identity/expression."[19] In addition to making a public team commitment to live the values of respect and inclusion for all team members, sports teams accepting this challenge treat all teammates with respect, avoid language that puts someone down because of differences, remind teammates that name-calling and bullying are not acceptable, and set an example of respect for opposing teams, fans, and other students in a school.[20]

The GLSEN Sports Project, though it only targets scholastic sports, is a great starting point for all youth programs, since it contains all of the elements considered necessary for inclusiveness as determined by experts in the field. For example, an extremely well-received 2006 study asked over eight hundred diversity educators their opinions on the behaviors necessary for success with diverse demographics. The study tallied fifteen different behaviors, and these were aggregated into four distinct categories:

1. We must be willing to confront bias, both our own and those of other people.
2. We must take a proactive attempt to understand other cultures.
3. We must treat others with respect.
4. We must act inclusively (i.e., be willing to include diverse demographic groups in all areas of programming).[21]

A successful youth program prepares young people for successful adulthood, and in our multicultural world, this includes acknowledging and respecting the multifarious populations who exist side by side with each and every one of us. Interacting and cooperating with people who are different from us is a necessary ingredient for success. In fact, studies find that individuals who learn how to navigate between different cultures develop more cognitive complexity and emotional maturity, including confidence, self-esteem, flexibility, tolerance, increased problem-solving ability, and effective communication skills.

What responsible parents, whatever the status of their sexuality, would be anything less than thrilled to watch their children mature into adults with such skills and competencies?

8

Religious Institutions

On the cloudless day of May 24, 2011, representatives from thirty religious traditions in the United States assembled for a press conference in front of the White House as part of the annual Clergy Call for Justice and Equality sponsored by the Human Rights Campaign. Religious leaders representing the United Methodist Church, the Unitarian Universalist Church, the Metropolitan Community Church, the Episcopal Church, the Presbyterian Church, the Union for Reformed Judaism, and the United Church of Christ described their experiences and goals in working with LGBT individuals, and a focus on social justice was clear in all of the speeches. During the next hour, these leaders called for the repeal of the Defense of Marriage of Act, the implementation of the Employment Non-Discrimination Act, and a focus on LGBT youth bullying. As stated by Reverend Winnie Varghese of the Episcopal Church, "We believe that it can be safe to go to school, possible to find work based on your abilities, and possible to create a family as you choose. These are some of the basic building blocks of a fair society that respects the dignity of us all."[1] The thirty denominations represented at this three-day event are the spiritual homes of millions of American citizens.

Unfortunately, there are still numerous organized religions and communities of faith that condemn LGBTs and are the spiritual homes of millions of other Americans. For example, the American Baptist Church USA has over 5,500 local congregations consisting of 1.3 million members in the United States and Puerto Rico. It promulgates the belief that homosexuality "is incompatible with Christian teaching."[2] However, it does allow for future exploration and dialogue on the topic.

In contrast, Pentecostal denominations, the fastest-growing faith community in the world, are generally openly hostile to sexual minorities. Most have doctrinal statements condemning homosexuality. One such example is the International Pentecostal Holiness Church's statement: "We have maintained a strong position against premarital, extramarital, and deviant sex, including homosexual and lesbian relationships, refusing to accept the loose moral standards of our society. We commit ourselves to maintaining this disciplined lifestyle with regard to our bodies."[3]

The Catholic Church in particular has been singled out for its treatment of LGBTs. Catholicism is the largest Christian denomination in the United States and has approximately 62 million members. While the Catholic Church does not consider homosexuality to be a sin in itself, *acting* on these sexual impulses is considered sinful. Gay men and lesbians are expected to remain celibate for their entire lives. The Catholic Church, while condemning prejudicial and discriminatory treatment of sexual minorities, simultaneously rejects marriage rights for same-sex couples and adoption by LGBT parents. The Church has not exhibited timidity or diffidence in obtaining these ends. It entreats congregants to oppose legislation promoting marriage and parental rights for sexual minorities; in 2003, four Massachusetts bishops sent a letter to all Catholic pastors in the state mandating them to read a statement during Sunday services that denounced marriage rights for same-sex couples.[4] The Catholic Church also vilifies politicians willing to support gay rights. In 2004, several Catholic bishops announced that they would refuse communion to politicians who failed to adhere to the church's stand on marriage rights for same-sex couples.[5]

With such a history, it seems that two lesbian mothers' discouraging experience with a Catholic school in 2010 was inevitable. The two women, both physicians who wished to remain anonymous in spite of the media attention surrounding their case, were members of the Sacred Heart of Jesus Parish in Boulder, Colorado. In an interview, they described themselves as "practicing Catholics eager to raise their children in the faith of their parents and grandparents."[6] They attended mass weekly and had their two children enrolled in the parish school. When they enrolled their oldest daughter in 2008, they made no attempt to hide their relationship from school administrators and teachers. They even offered to go elsewhere if their relationship posed a problem, but were told it made no difference. And for three years, no issue seemed to have surfaced. Then, in 2010, upon submitting an application for their youngest daughter to re-enroll in preschool, one of the mothers was ominously summoned to the principal's office. "She sat me down and told me we were no longer accepted here any more. She said it was not going to be a good fit for our child and that she would encourage us to look elsewhere. . . . Her main point was she was concerned about our child, about her well-being. She never came out and said we were not welcomed to stay. But she pretty much told us it was time for us to move on."[7]

Father William Breslin, the pastor of the Sacred Heart Parish, responded to criticism of the decision by explaining, "The issue is not about our not accepting 'sinners.' It is not about punishing the child for the sins of his or her parents. It is simply that the lesbian couple is saying that their relationship is a good one that should be accepted by everyone; and the church cannot agree to that."[8] This was echoed in a statement by Denver archbishop Charles Chaput: "Parents of Catholic school students are expected to agree with church beliefs, including those forbidding sex between anyone other than married, heterosexual couples. Catholic schools work as religious partners with parents . . . parents are expected to support the Catholic mission of the school."[9] It is difficult to see how LGBT parents can support a Catholic mission that equates same-sex parenting with "doing violence to these children" as described in the Vatican's *Congregation for the Doctrine of the Faith*?[10]

Recent statistics on the state of religion in the United States inform us that 92 percent of Americans believe in God or some form of higher power, 43.1 percent of Americans report weekly or almost weekly church attendance, and that non-Catholic Christians—the largest religious group in the country today—are heavily concentrated in the South and nearby states, while constituting only a minority of residents of Northeastern states, and of many Middle Atlantic and Western states.[11] How are LGBT families handling the conflicts that abound in their efforts to instill a religious and spiritual upbringing for their children?

Choice One: Cutting Ties

In 1964, Don Lucas, executive secretary of the Mattachine Society, sent out 150 surveys regarding the demographics of the gay men comprising its national mailing list. One question was, "What denomination, if any, were you raised in and what influence, good or bad, did it have on your childhood or now?" Forty written responses were received. While many mentioned the positive influences their religious upbringing offered them, such as instilling moral principles, fostering a relationship with a higher power, and providing social gatherings, many also reported the less salubrious effects of a spiritual upbringing in an organized religion. One respondent, a sixteen-year-old boy, wrote, "How am I supposed to know what my creator thinks of me? The Church says that God thinks I am a 'monster.' Throughout my whole life I've received the sacraments, done good things and bad things, sinned and confessed. Now—since a couple months ago, I am 'against nature,' which is the law of God, and 'unless you don't change you are doomed' . . . I don't want to be condemned. . . . Please don't make me feel I'll go straight to Hell—at least send me to Purgatory, then I'll have a slight chance to progress."[12]

Fortunately, over the past twenty years we have witnessed astounding progress in several denominations' responses to LGBT worshippers, but many continue to direct messages of shame, hate, and intolerance to the these individuals who are closeted in their spiritual communities. In 2009, a joint collaboration between the National Gay and Lesbian Task Force's Institute for Welcoming Resources, COLAGE, and Family Equality Council produced *All in God's Family: Creating Allies for Our LGBT Families*, a curriculum designed to help faith communities support and embrace LGBT people and their families. The document makes no effort to obfuscate the state of organized religion for these families:

> In the past, it was almost impossible for a person to find a church in which to be supported, challenged, and loved as an openly LGBT disciple on a sacred journey. In twenty years much has changed... [T]here is much to be grateful for and there is much more to be accomplished. LGBT persons are still not embraced in spiritual sanctuaries across the country. Instead of words of welcome, they hear words of condemnation and insult from the lips of the very people from whom they expect and deserve love, support, and spiritual leadership. They hear themselves equated with pedophiles and criminals. They hear their loving relationships described in terms of bestial acts. They watch while their spiritual leaders lobby aggressively against their human and civil rights.[13]

It's not surprising that the most common response I encounter in regard to the spiritual involvement of LGBTs is their complete abandonment of the practices of their upbringing, often the abandonment of faith-based practices entirely. If people have been told for decades that they are "monsters," shameful in the sight of God, unlovable, and detestable, it is no wonder that so many have simply stop believing in a loving higher power. Joe Kort, one of country's experts on gay-affirmative counseling, has written that religion is one of the worst arenas for sexuality abuse.[14] I have found in my own clinical work that many LGBT families seeking help for substance abuse issues—whether adult or the child is the identified patient—will willingly engage in family treatment, a necessary treatment option, but refuse to take part in a twelve-step program, even if only on a trial basis, because two of the twelve steps specifically dictate the acceptance of the role of a higher power in one's life.

Jacob was raised in the Catholic Church and went through twelve years of Catholic schooling. The last day he attended a church service of any type (other than inescapable weddings and funerals) was in high school. Now, eighteen years later, he never looks back: "I have no regrets. The Catholic Church fucked me up, and really they should be prosecuted for the emotional abuse they put me through. At this point in my life, I don't believe in a god or a higher power or any such thing." When I asked him about how he approaches this with his adopted children, he told me, "They know about my experiences growing up and my antipathy and condemnation of religion, but they have the freedom to choose what they want. I told them jokingly I might become suicidal if they were opt for Catholicism or some fundamental evangelical sect, but if they want to seek an organized religion when they are older, who am I to stop them? But for now we have a purely secular household."

Choice Two: Joining a New Church

In 1968, Troy Perry announced the first service of his new church in the *Advocate*. This service, which would eventually evolve into the Metropolitan Community Church, attracted twelve people on the night of its debut. That night, Perry stated that though his church would serve the needs of the homosexual community, it was a Christian church, *not a gay church*. Perry fully expected the MCC to be on an equal footing with other denominations but open to anyone, particularly those believers estranged from the dominant, traditional, organized religions.

Perry's long personal journey to the establishment of MCC was a history of efforts to work within the confines of the Pentecostal and Baptist religions in which he had been reared. However, his repeated attempts to change or at least manage his sexuality were ultimately unsuccessful and led to his realization that a new church was needed. Perry's evolution from a devout proponent of traditional organized religion to the inevitable recognition that a rapprochement between his church's tenets and his sexuality was impossible is a common theme in the lives of LGBT parents.

Perry's struggle still plays out in the daily lives of LGBTs. A church, the focal point for so many people's lives, does not have to be a welcoming place. Consider the 2005 sermon delivered by Reverend Willie Wilson of the Union Temple Baptist Church, in which he preached that lesbians were one of the primary reasons for problems in the African American community: "We live in a time when our brothers have been so put down, can't get a job, lots of sisters making more money than brothers. And it's creating problems in families. That's one of the reasons our families breaking up. And that's one of the reasons many of our women are becoming lesbians. You got to be careful when you say you don't need no man, I can make it by myself. Well, if you don't need a man, what's left? Lesbianism is about to take over our community."[15]

Yet such sentiments do not always lead LGBT families to abandon religion altogether. Joining another church or organized religion is the answer for many LGBT families, at least those who have the option of other churches from which to choose from. Peg, a Christian living in Mississippi, doesn't look back with regret or anger at the years she spent closeted as a member of an evangelical church. "The anti-gay vehemence in my church had definitely declined, and it was uncommon for the pastor to attack us in comparison to the past. Don't get me wrong . . . our service couldn't in any way be called 'inviting,' but it became a lot easier for me to sit through. When our pastor did erupt into his attacks, I would remind my son that that was his opinion. But things had quieted down. Then when Obama took office and started making changes, the whole 'gay rights' efforts whipped up a firestorm. Enough is enough, I told myself. We joined a Presbyterian church."

Peg defended her former church even though she was no longer a member. She was clear that there were many members there who would not have been aghast or disapproving at learning she was a lesbian; she was certain that they would have come to her aid. But coming out would have focused too much attention on her and her son and forced a dialogue among the congregants that she didn't believe many were ready to undertake. She admitted that she ultimately enabled her church by remaining a hidden minority; her fellow congregants were able to elide the topic rather than confront the antigay comments by the preacher. If she had remained childless, she might still be a member of the church, but with a four-year-old son in tow, hearing messages of hate, even if they occurred rarely, was too much.

Choice Three: Working from Within

While some LGBTs have forsaken organized religion altogether and others have moved onto more welcoming denominations, some intrepid individuals have made it their task to force open the doors of the resistant churches to which they have long been affiliated. A historic example is Pat Nidorf, ordained as a Catholic priest in 1962 but also the founder of DignityUSA in 1969. Like Troy Perry, he advertised for gay Catholics in the gay newspapers and was soon alternating meetings between San Diego and Los Angeles. In 1971, Nidorf sent a letter to the archdiocese asking for official recognition of the group. In response, he was ordered to stop his work. Undeterred, he began a national outreach campaign. At the time of writing, DignityUSA has chapters throughout the United States.

Dignity clearly states it "advocates for change in the Catholic Church's teaching on homosexuality."[16] Its services are unabashedly Catholic and include the sacraments. Mark Jordan, professor of divinity at the Harvard Divinity School and author of *Recruiting Young Love: How Christians Talk About Sexuality*, explains that "MCC is in ways a separatist model. . . . Dignity by contrast is a model of working from within. . . . Except that Dignity was never really incorporated into Catholic structures."[17] More than forty years after Dignity's founding, the Catholic Church refuses to recognize it. Nevertheless, as outgoing president Mark Matson wrote in 2011, "In 42 years of nearly constant repression, the leadership of the Roman Catholic Church has been unable to pull us down."[18]

In *Living Openly in Your Place of Worship*, its resource for LGBTs contemplating coming out to their respective churches, the Human Rights Campaign offers four reasons to engage in this often-intimidating process:[19]

1. To affirm the whole of you
2. To help your congregation grow in love and compassion

3. To change the conversation about GLBT people of faith

4. To build religious institutions that are true to their missions and values

LGBT activist and leader Sue Hyde took the confrontational approach. As noted earlier, during the 2004 debate over same-sex marriage in Massachusetts, four implacable Catholic bishops asked parish priests to read a letter asking that parishioners vote to ban same-sex marriage. Hyde took action:

I could not allow this letter to be delivered at my neighborhood church without any response. . . . I attended Mass on Sunday morning, February 8, 2004. After the priest read the letter, I stood up in a pew and said, "Forgive me, Father, I have sinned many times since my last Confession thirty-five years ago. I live across the street with my partner and our two children. Our kids attend public school with some of the children of this parish. I want you to know that my family wishes no harm to your families. I ask that you respect our family as we respect yours. Please do not support the constitutional amendment that would exclude our family from the protections and responsibilities granted through marriage. We only want to take care of each other in the best way we can, just as you do. Thank you and God bless."[20]

Hyde admits, "Not all of us would be able to interrupt the presiding priest at a Catholic Mass."[21] Many take a more diffident approach. Donald, for example, had been attending Baptist services in Baltimore for more than a decade. He told me he was living the "down low" for all those years. After beginning his first relationship with a male partner though, he quickly recognized his own "stuff" would lead to its death and the likelihood that he would be unable to engage in any meaningful same-sex relationship. He began counseling with a very affirmative mental health worker. Later, after sitting through yet another service in which sexual minorities were excoriated, particularly gay men, he recognized he had had enough. He practiced approaching his pastor with his partner and carefully asking him to refrain from or at least tone down the homonegative rhetoric. He wasn't ready to out himself, though:

> I approached him after the service when he was in his study. I told him that since beginning college [as an older student], I had encountered several gay men, and none of them had a resemblance to the sex-crazed disease-spreading monsters he was promoting from his pulpit. I also told him that maybe "we" should be a little more restrained in demonizing gay men because for all we know there could be some sitting in our church's pews. I don't think he suspected that I was in any way talking about myself, and he told me that returning to school was certainly putting some "novel ideas" in my head. But he reminded me that his mission was to save souls, and that if there were gay men in the congregation, hearing the truth about God's disapproval was the surest way to salvation. It was obvious he wasn't going to stop. In fact, during the next service he informed us that "several people" had approached him about his treatment of gay men in his sermons; he respectfully didn't single me out. He said that he apologized if he was offensive, but it was certainly better to be offended now and have one's eyes opened to the damnation that was otherwise awaiting.

Donald ultimately left his church. "It was hard," he reflected. "These people were my family. They were there when my mother died. They were there when my brother died. They threw a surprise party for my graduation. I still miss them. But I couldn't do it any more." He and his partner and their son are part of a Presbyterian congregation in which their relationship is known to all.

An obsessively negative focus on LGBTs is understandable when a denomination holds that this is a way to "save souls," but many churches also refrain from becoming more open because there is a fear that such treatment of LGBTs will lead to conflict and divisiveness within the congregation and possibly provoke members to depart for less-tolerant churches. In this they are mistaken. A 2009 study examined the impact of becoming more welcoming of sexual minorities on 364 churches across the country.[22] Only 7 percent of the respondents indicated that their congregants had difficultly talking openly about LGBT issues. Less than a third (29 percent) reported any significant conflict within the congregation within the last two years, and among these, the most common sources of conflict were pastoral leadership, finances, and worship, not homosexuality or gender identity. Finally, nearly three-quarters of the respondents disagreed with these statements: "Our congregation risks losing members by talking too much about homosexuality" (73 percent) and "Becoming more welcoming to LGBT persons could hinder our congregation's ability to reach racial/ethnic minorities" (72 percent).

Rather than the expected conflict, the study found, welcoming congregations "exhibit lower levels of conflict, in general and on issues of LGBT concerns than other congregations."[23] These finding are similar to those of another survey, which found that just 34 percent of progressive clergy reported that their congregations had experienced any significant conflict over the last two years. For these clergy, the primary sources of conflict were pastoral leadership (cited by 57 percent), finances (42 percent), building/grounds (21 percent), and worship (20 percent). Homosexuality was cited by only twenty-one clergy members (16 percent of respondents to the question).[24]

As more and more organized religions officially welcome and advocate for LGBTs, we will be left with a small but strident group who militantly oppose welcoming and acceptance (unless predicated on efforts to actively change LGBT members' sexuality or convince them to remain celibate). This stance is based on their religious precepts and on the belief that to become more welcoming will be deleterious in the long run. In the 2009 survey, 36 percent of clergy affirmed, "Our congregation risks losing many members by talking too much about homosexuality."[25] Even so, some sexual minorities remain in intolerant and even homonegative communities of faith, working to improve them from the inside, though as the example of Dignity clearly illustrates, acceptance may be a long time in coming.

Solution Four: Living in the Church Closet

A 2011 study examined the process by which LGBT individuals with a Christian upbringing resolved the conflict between sexual identity and religious beliefs.[26] It found that this conflict typically led to three initial responses: depression, increased secrecy, and more intense religious involvement. The participants in the study were fortunately able to eventually work through this conflict, but their experiences shouldn't be taken as the norm.

Lee, who lives in Mississippi, told me of her dream of moving to Jacksonville, Florida. She had read that the city was now considered one of the "gayest in the Bible Belt" and the home to eight accepting churches. At present, though, the thought of relocation was unrealistic. For Lee, a single mother with a high-school education and working a minimal-wage position, Jacksonville remains a tantalizing but elusive goal. Lee is a Southern Baptist, a denomination that vehemently condemns LGBTs; she is also an avid church attendee.

"I don't have a choice," she informed me. "There are several Christian churches I could easily attend. Believe me, there is no shortage of churches in my town. But the message about my lifestyle will be the same no matter which one I go to. Being lesbian is immoral; I rank *down* there with pornography and adultery. As for coming out, even to the people I know are open-minded, forget it. Once word got around . . . and this is a small, small town—word will get around—I'll be out of job the very next day."

Lee seemed to be struggling to maintain her composure at this point, so I asked if she wanted to continue. She assented. I wanted to know how she managed to reconcile her church's ongoing assault on her sexuality with her role as a single lesbian mother:

> I'm lesbian because I'm attracted to other women. But really I'm celibate; I haven't been sexually involved with anybody in half a decade. My son's father is out of our lives, so for all intents and purposes I am a single mom. When our pastor lets loose with his fire-and-brimstone

speeches on homosexuality, my son [a seven year old] is often in attendance. To him, a gay man or a lesbian woman is someone to be feared,
scorned, and pitied, often all at the same time. He has no idea of my
identity, and, at his age, he really shouldn't.

I asked her what she thought about the implications of her choices:

I don't really have choices right now. Would I rather be honest with
my son? Of course I would. But what if he accidently slipped in school
and disclosed his mother is a lesbian? What if he told his most trusted
friend, who then turned out to be not so trustworthy? We'll both be
tormented, and I'll be out of work.

The 2008 report *Living Openly in Your Place of Worship* discusses
why LGBTs delay coming out to their faith communities.[27] These are
the most common reasons:

- *Rejection:* Coming out to fellow congregants risks negative reac-
  tions, particularly in places of worship notable for their condemnation of LGBTs. This is even more perilous if neighbors, family
  members, and coworkers attend the same church.
- *Jeopardizing other aspects of one's life:* Coming out to one's congregation will likely lead to others learning of this disclosure, including those who have no affiliation with the place of worship.
  It is likely that employers, family members, and neighbors will
  also soon learn of this revelation.
- *Other important issues are occurring simultaneously:* Coming out
  to one's place of worship when undergoing other stressors may
  only make the disclosure experience more anxiety-provoking.
  Ironically, times of duress are the times when fellow worshippers
  are most valuable in one's life.

The report reminded readers, "In some cases, the emotional and
spiritual costs of being open in a particular faith community may be
too high."

Some LGBTs, particularly those living in urban and suburban areas, have a cornucopia of welcoming faith-based institutions from which to choose, while others have none that support their family composition. Still, many LGBTs I spoke with continued to attend services in homonegative churches even when other options were available. There seemed to be three reasons for this choice. First, many had invested years in a particular church; their fellow parishioners and congregants were their support system and "family"—the men and women they turned to in times of strife and duress, as long as it didn't involve issues related to their sexuality. Second, joining another church was certain to lead to questions and might inadvertently "out" them. Finally, the homonegative messages inculcated in these places of worship were consistent with their own beliefs.

Eddie, an African American gay father who has joint custody of his son from a former marriage, considers his church to be his community. He is more than welcome in his church in spite of its denunciations of homosexuality, because he is trying to "turn straight." Though this has not yet happened (and he privately disclosed to me that it might never) he is at least now celibate. "I was driving down to rest stops along the Interstate and hanging out in my car for hours waiting for some sign from a perfect stranger that he might be interested in oral sex. It was horrible, and I don't want to go through that ever again. I was lying to the people I love for years. When I finally came out to my wife, she didn't handle it too well. She told her family and then, in a small community like ours, the news spread like wildfire."

The pastor and elders of the church soon engaged in a reconnaissance mission and surprised Eddie one night in his new apartment. They were there to save his soul—and this was also what he wanted. Eddie states that as long as he is making efforts to change his life around (i.e., to become non-gay) he is a welcome member of his church. "People pray for me just like they pray for those afflicted by alcoholism, drug addiction, and other diseases." He glowingly described an idyllic church picnic in which he sat and laughed with his fellow congregants while his son played with their children: "There I was surrounded by people who care for me, both body and soul. Nobody was throwing stones at me because we all recognize we live in glass houses. I'm working on my problem, and they know and respect it. This is my community."

Some readers may be aghast at Eddie's choices, but we must recognize that in the community of gay parents, we must make room for a diversity of beliefs and experiences. And though he describes himself as an "unwillingly gay parent," Eddie loves his son and has no regrets regarding his role as a father.

It's easy to slip into black-and-white thinking about intolerant churches, but there are always forces of resistance present, even if muted. Monica, who now attends a MCC after moving to New York from Nebraska, fondly remembers an older woman who approached her after a particularly vehement antigay sermon in her church. "'What a bunch of bullshit,' she said to me. Did she know I was a lesbian? I certainly wasn't out in my community. But I knew then and there that there were people who understood." It is in these moments of support that so many LGBTs find sustaining relationships in denominations that, at least on the surface, don't tolerate them. Interviewees implored me to remind readers that even in the most outwardly antigay churches, there are and always have been pockets of resistance.

Intolerance in "Welcoming" Churches

Believe Out Loud describes itself as "a collection of clergy and lay leaders, LGBT activists, and concerned individuals, working together to help the Protestant community become more welcoming to gays and lesbians."[28] As part of its campaign of inclusiveness, it released a video in 2011 showing two lesbian mothers and their son entering a new church. As they slowly advance down the aisle, they become the recipients of unfriendly or confused stares and laughter; at one point, they are even pointed at. It all ends on a positive note, though, when the male preacher smiles and then, looking at them directly, says, "Welcome . . . everyone." The relieved family enters a pew, members of a new church community. Or are they?

Over the last decade, church leaders came to recognize that even their denomination's statements regarding inclusiveness were not necessarily accepted and acted on in individual congregations. The "welcoming churches" movement emerged, in which groups such as Believe Out Loud and the Institute for Welcoming Resources, launched efforts to help these congregations discuss issues regarding sexuality and "transform your lives, your congregation, and your world into a loving place in which God's lesbian, gay, bisexual, and transgender (LGBT) families can thrive."[29]

Some of the methods used to nurture a welcoming environment include reading a welcoming statement within the first five minutes of a service acknowledging LGBT members, offering Sunday school lessons focused on LGBT issues, offering space to PFLAG or Soulforce meetings, collecting special offerings for LGBT causes, and having the church participate in a pride parade. Some church leaders and congregants, however, have found these behaviors too progressive and even bordering on activism. Carol, for example, taught Sunday school for her Presbyterian church. One of the boys attending had gay fathers.

LGBT bullying was in the headlines, and one of the children in my Sunday school class was being bullied because of her weight. After talking about her plight, I asked how children with two mothers or fathers might be bullied and how they might cope. I never mentioned Jacob's name during the class, but the children knew he had two fathers. I thought our session went really well, but I received a phone call from the pastor, who told me that some parents had complained I was teaching about gay and lesbian issues, concerns they thought should not be included in a Sunday school. This shocked me. How inclusive is a church in which we can't address one of the most pressing issues encountering gay and lesbian youth?

We have seen how many LGBTs belonging to intolerant communities of faith who seek solace in a small number of fellow congregants who are welcoming and who eschew formal church doctrine. Carol's experience is the converse; she was a member of an ostensibly welcoming church with pockets of resistance to LGBT presence. Not all members of "welcoming" churches will necessarily be welcoming.

✦ ✦ ✦

LGBT families partake of religious services ranging from those in churches that remain implacable foes to LGBTs to those offered by the Metropolitan Community Church, specifically founded to meet the spiritual needs of the LGBT communities. Throughout all of this, we cannot forget the needs of the involved children. Adult LGBTs can weight the pros and cons of their adopted religious venue, but their children often have little choice as to which service to attend and have less cognitive prowess to dissect the messages of hate from the positive messages and prescriptions that a congregation can offer.

This was a tough issue for Lee, introduced above, who hid her sexuality from both her church and her child. She worried about the wedge this might create between herself and her son: "After having sit through years of these antigay messages in church, can I ever come out to him? How will I explain this to him years from now?" These questions are applicable to all LGBT parents who belong to denominations that proscribe homosexuality. What is the impact of the child's view of homosexuality? How will it impact a relationship with a parent or parents? And if a child is aware of a parent's sexuality, how does it impact him or her to collude to keep this hidden from the congregation?

It would seem easier to simply join a welcoming church (recognizing that even welcoming churches have their limits as to acceptance), but for many, this isn't possible when there are no better options. Others are too heavily invested in their current congregation to consider changing.

Inclusion of LGBT families in religious denominations is a fairly new issue, though they have been attending services quietly for centuries. Most of the focus has been on LGBT adults, and the addition of children complicates the process and our understanding of what is the best for all.

9
The Legal System

Christopher Rudow. Troy Martinez Clattenberg. Amanda Gonzalez-Andujar. Brian Betts. Chanel Larkin. Paul Michalik. Victoria Carmen White. These names may be unfamiliar to most readers, but they are just a few of the victims of the twenty-seven known murders of LGBTs occurring in 2010, which, according to the National Coalition of Anti-Violence Programs (NCAVP), is the second highest total since it starting tracking this data in 1998.[1] While some were murdered by strangers, many knew their killers. Consider the case of Courtney Bright, a twenty-four-year-old woman whose body was found in a foreclosed house in Lakeland, Florida. She had been strangled by the father of her girlfriend of three years, allegedly because he disapproved of their relationship. The death of Roy Antonio Jones of Southampton, New York, received national attention: he was sixteen months old when he was beaten to death by his mother's boyfriend, who was trying to make him act like a boy rather than a girl.

The NCAVP doesn't just track murders; this coalition of seventeen antiviolence programs, working in fifteen states, also collects data regarding violence against LGBTs. It reported that in 2010 such violence increased by 13 percent.[2] Sharon Stapel of the New York Anti-Violence Project, one of the collaborating agencies, me that in spite of the NCAVP's glowing reputation for measuring and responding to anti-LGBT violence, its statistics "are only the tip of the iceberg." The coalition doesn't collect data for thirty-five states, so "[t]here's a lot more violence against [LGBT] and HIV-affected people than we know about."[3]

In regard to violence against LGBT families, we only have anecdotal evidence; the research to date doesn't give us an idea of how much is occurring and whether it is increasing or decreasing. Nobody doubts it is occurring, though. Mitch is an unfortunate example of its existence. While living in Kentucky, he and his partner left their two-year-old son with a babysitter recommended by several parents in the neighborhood in order to attend a colleague's birthday party. Mitch and Joe had never hidden their status as same-sex parents, though they did not flagrantly advertise it; discretion was their modus operandi. While they were out, the babysitter invited several friends over, who proceeded to explore off-limits areas of their home. Obviously, they came across evidence of their relationship, because only two days later a campaign of torment began—threatening phone calls, the word "fag" scratched into their car, windows shattered, and a letter demanding that they give up their son to a "normal family" or they would take him by force. Even though they had only recently moved to this suburb to escape the toxic environment of the city, they now believed they were in more danger than at any other point in their lives. The family relocated once again, this time back to the city.

An intolerant community can be a threatening environment where parents, children, property, and even pets can become the focus of community ire or the antipathy of only a few members whose actions are silently condoned by their more circumspect neighbors. This active intolerance can take many forms, including bullying, threats and family intimidation, physical harm, damage to property, and deliberate attempts to make a community as unwelcoming and inhospitable to targeted gay families. The clear message: "Get out."

Many LGBT families live in communities that shun, denigrate, and even attempt to expel them. While some rural areas take a live and let live approach, others support verbal homonegative attacks, violence, and hate crimes. It's important to remember that small-town America is not the only unwelcoming neighborhood; many residential neighborhoods in large cities are also wracked with homophobia and seething intolerance. For example, the 2007 report *Our Families: Attributes of Bay Area Lesbian, Gay, Bisexual & Transgender Parents and Their Children* found that even in the heterogeneous San Francisco Bay area, "with its substantial LGBT presence and history of a strong, visible, and public LGBT community, LGBT families struggle against exclusion and isolation. This may be especially true if a family encompasses multiple minority identities and faces multiple forms of discrimination. LGBT parents particularly struggle to protect the physical and emotional safety of their children and themselves in this environment. LGBT families frequently experience discrimination—and sometimes harassment—in daycare and school settings, medical settings, at the playground, in religious communities, in their neighborhoods, and even within their own extended families."[4]

The National Gay and Lesbian Task Force introduced the first national LGBT antiviolence program in 1982 with an emphasis on both quantifying this violence and mobilizing the community to end the mistreatment of sexual minorities.[5] Nevertheless, thirty years later, accurate data is difficult to obtain. According to Gregory Herek, one of the country's leading experts on sexual-minority violence, criminal acts against LGBTs are widespread, but relevant data regarding these acts is fragmentary.[6]

It was hoped that the 2009 Matthew Shepard and James Byrd, Jr. Hate Crimes Prevention Act (HCPA) would improve the collection of data. The Act requires the FBI to track and publish the number of hate crimes reported by law enforcement departments to their respective states. However, underreporting is a serious concern. In 2009, 85.9 percent of the participating agencies reported zero hate crimes in their jurisdictions. In addition, thousands of police agencies across the nation did not provide statistics at all—including at least five agencies in cities with populations of more than 250,000 and at least thirteen agencies in cities with populations between 100,000 and 250,000. Because of these problems with reporting, the FBI's *Hate Crimes Statistics Report* fails to cover approximately 30 million Americans.[7]

Another source of hate-crimes reporting is the National Crime Victimization Survey (NCVS), a survey of a nationally representative sample of persons age twelve or older in US households. Each year victim self-reports capture information about the number and characteristics of victimizations, both reported *and not reported* to law enforcement. A 2011 Bureau of Justice Statistics report measuring hate crimes occurring between 2003 and 2009 and measured via the NCVS found that in contrast to the six- to ten thousand cases per year in this time frame captured by FBI tracking, the NCVS determined that an average of *169,000* such cases occurred per year during this same time period.[8] According to Jack McDevitt, hate-crimes expert and criminology professor at Northeastern University, surveys of households "are considered more accurate than those reported by police departments—in part, because they include crimes never reported to authorities."[9]

Avoiding the Police

Both the NCVS and FBI acknowledge that police are notified in fewer than half (45 percent) of all hate-crime victimizations. Additional evidence supporting this conclusion comes from a 2010 study by Queers for Economic Justice, which found that 45 percent of survey respondents relied on themselves alone when facing legal problems.[10] Furthermore, the 2011 NCAVP's annual report that found that 50 percent of LGBT individuals did not report an incident of discrimination, and harassment.[11]

Turning to the police or other law enforcement officials is often inconceivable for LGBT families. Why?

During the writing of this book, I was invited to the baby shower for a male couple and the surrogate who was soon to give birth to their child. While there, I was surrounded by numerous LGBT parents, many of whom took an interest in the topic of the book. I asked them how they would handle a hate crime or some other form of community harassment or discrimination. The responses were not surprising, since they were coming from a niche demographic of LGBT parents—white, affluent, and living in an urban area. The most common responses, in descending order, were: call the police; call the media (particularly the local gay newspaper); contact one of the national activist legal organizations such as Lambda Legal or the Human Rights Campaign; and, if necessary, obtain legal counsel.

Several months later, I was sharing dinner with Adelle and Eva in their small home on the outskirts of Branson, Missouri, in the Ozark Mountains. They had sent their children to a friend's for the evening so that we could talk undisturbed. Though neither had experienced a hate crime or could recall any overtly homonegative comment or behavior since high school—many years ago—they were still "playing it safe" by declining to out themselves and their relationship to neighbors, who, I assumed, were very few in number, given their rural location. Still, I posed the same question I had asked the shower attendees: How would you handle a hate crime?

"We would hope," said Adelle, speaking for both of them, "that it was an isolated incident. We would ignore it unless it became really threatening."

"What about the police?" I asked.

They simultaneously grimaced.

"Not unless it was a really life-threatening situation."

Such reluctance to seek the help of police was echoed in a conversation I had with Gabriel, a single gay father living in Oklahoma. He had already served time in prison for possession of drugs: "Though I served less than two years, I never want to go through that again. A gay man should *never* be placed in a prison with straight men. Never. Make sure you quote me on that. I hid being gay for the entire time I was involved in prison, from my arrest even till now with my current probation officer. Gay men were tortured by the guards and the inmates . . . 'tortured' is the right word. It was horrific. I hear people joke that gay men must like prison since it gives them free rein to horny men, but if they saw what actually happens to these guys they wouldn't joke about it anymore."

Gabriel is closeted. But he asserted that if he were out as a gay man he wouldn't contact the police for help. When I asked him why, he replied,

> First, I was in prison. If I call the police, I'll come under suspicion even if I am the victim of a crime. My history will always impact my ability to use the police—even the entire legal system. I can't count on being treated fairly. But it gets worse. If I needed the police for a hate crime or other violence against me, I cannot assume the responding officer isn't going to act out their prejudices on me. Do you know how many gay men I met while in prison who were roughed up by the police? The homophobic shit I heard the guards say again and again only reinforced how dangerous contact with the "authorities" can be if you're a gay man. I would handle problems on my own. And if that meant moving, then so be it.

Finally, in Flagstaff, Arizona, I had arranged a lunch with Bruce and Samuel. However, only Bruce, looking contrite and exasperated, arrived. He apologized: "I'm so sorry. Sam got spooked. Arizona already has draconian immigration laws, but then John McCain blamed immigrants for starting the fire that blazed through here several months ago. Sam felt that talking to you might put him in some type of danger. After all, he is undocumented."

Bruce was such a relaxed and entertaining conversationalist that I could have easily spent our entire hour together listening to his life story. He had met Samuel at a club, and though it wasn't love at first sight, it was passionate sex followed by the gradual development of love. He had joint custody of his son from a former marriage, and he was hoping that his son and Samuel would bond. I too asked him about involving police in his life. "I wouldn't hesitate to call the police, but I've been told that I have white male privilege. Sam could never involve the police; it might have legal repercussions for him. When you're a gay undocumented immigrant living in a state that promotes violence against both identities, you learn to solve problems on your own. That's one of the reasons Sam is closeted." David Stocum, executive director of the New Mexico GLBTQ Centers, shared a similar sentiment: "Our state is primarily Latino. If a person is undocumented and he or she is experiencing some type of problem in the community—hate crimes included—they go to the family or they go to the church. They don't go to the police."[12]

Immigration laws compound the complexities already encountered by families such as Bruce and Samuel's. US citizens and permanent residents are allowed to sponsor a foreign-born spouse or fiancé(e) for entry into the United States, but only if their partner is of the opposite sex. DOMA prevents the federal government from recognizing the marriages of same-sex couples. As a result, LGBT Americans cannot sponsor a same-sex partner, even if the couple is legally married in their state. As a result, children of same-sex, binational couples face the constant threat of losing a parent through deportation or denial of a visa. If the child of a same-sex, binational couple is foreign-born and if his or her American parent cannot become a legal parent, that parent also cannot sponsor the child for immigration purposes. Therefore, the child may be deported regardless of how long he or she has lived in the United States. Similarly, if the American partner of a foreign-born parent wants to secure ties to their children through a second-parent adoption, going through that process could put the foreign-born parent's status at risk if he or she is on a temporary visa or is undocumented. As summed up in the report *All Children Matter*, "The law pulls [LGBT] families in two different directions: they cannot secure legal parenting ties without risking their immigration status."[13]

Re-victimization

Historically, police have been seen not as supports for the community but rather as threats that enforced heterosexist hegemony. LGBT activist groups were infiltrated by the police. Clubs, bars, and bathhouses were targeted for raids, and the identities of patrons were made public. Arrests were more often than not replete with physical brutality and/

or harsh, derogatory, and shaming treatment. Unfortunately, similarly harsh treatment continues today.

According to a 2008 NCAVP report, for LGBTs, the "average police response . . . is often cited . . . as a re-victimizing experience."[14] In a 2005 report, Amnesty International (AI) found that "LGBT people often do not report crimes against them, in particular hate crimes and domestic violence, because they are reluctant to reveal their sexual orientation or gender identity to responding officers, and because they fear homophobic or transphobic treatment at the hands of police officers"[15] Even the US Department of Justice advised policymakers, "Some victims have little confidence that authorities will bring the perpetrators to justice."[16]

Alexia, a lesbian woman in her forties, sought help from the NCAVP in 2010. In her words,

> I was at a bar with my brother and his boyfriend, and we got into an argument because I was trying to get my car keys back from my brother's boyfriend, who was verbally abusive—has been for many years with my brother—and was threatening to leave with my car. Two off-duty cops who were working at the bar intervened, one of them threatening to give me a DUI if I did not get off the property. I said "Why would you give me a DUI? I'm not driving." I was trying to call 911, when suddenly I was attacked physically, first by one, then two, and then four plainclothes cops, and bar bouncers. One of them tried to choke me with his knee on my throat, another tried to break my fingers. I was in a hospital for two days with those injuries. I am a single mom, and I have three kids. To top it all, the cops then filed a case against me, charging me with assault.[17]

Officers responding to a crime against LGBT individuals often focus their attention on the victim's sexual orientation, gender identity or expression, at times explicitly or implicitly blaming the victim for what happened to him or her.[18] Amnesty International found that masculine appearing women and gay men were not perceived by some law enforcement officers as requiring or deserving protection from violence.

Due to their discomfort with LGBTs, investigations by the police are cursory and superficial.[19] AI's other findings included the following:

- Numerous reports described officers being verbally abusive toward LGBT individuals, with officers frequently focusing on perceived sexual orientation, or gender identity or expression of individuals in a derogatory and demeaning manner.
- Police verbal abuse of LGBT individuals was frequently sexualized, in particular against lesbians and transgender individuals.
- Law enforcement officers engaged in physical abuse of LGBTs.
- Law enforcement officials engaged in sexual harassment and abuse of LGBTs, including rape, sexual assault, threatened sexual assault, sexual contact, as well as sexually explicit language and gestures.
- LGBT individuals were subjected to sexual abuse or harassment while in detention, at the hands of other detainees and, in some cases, by officers.
- Abuse and violence against LGBTs by the police was particularly pronounced for transgender individuals, LGBT people of color, youth, immigrants and homeless individuals.[20]

According to the NCAVP, in 2010, law enforcement officers were the fourth-largest category of perpetrators of anti-LGBT violence.[21] In their 2010 survey of low-income LGBTs, Queers for Economic Justice reported that 40 percent of respondents experienced discrimination from the police. Almost half of survey respondents reported having been arrested in the last two years, 29 percent had been strip-searched, and 19 percent had been physically assaulted.[22] And, as has been noted throughout this book, those who bear the brunt of hostile and homophobic treatment, in this case by the legal authorities, are often those with the least resources to fight back. Factors contributing to underreporting include fear of treatment based on race or ethnicity, age, immigration status, socioeconomic status, and language and cultural barriers; there is also fear of being arrested for participation in criminalized activity.

The authors of the book *Queer Injustice: The Criminalization of LGBT People in the United States* propose that understanding the differences in treatment for specific LGBT groups requires "discarding the facile notion that all queers experience the stigma of criminalization and the criminal legal system in the same ways. Queer engagement with law enforcement cannot be accurately described, much less analyzed, as a stand-alone, generic 'gay' experience because race, class, and gender are crucial factors in determining how and which queers will bear the brunt of violence at the hands of the criminal legal system."[23]

It is not surprising, then, that the NCAVP's annual report found that in 2010 60 percent of LGBTs individuals described police attitudes as indifferent, abusive, or a deterrent.[24]

Dangers in the Courts

Additionally, LGBTs have reason to be wary of the court system. Chris, a lesbian mother, told me that she had never felt unwelcome in her township in Richland County, Ohio. Community acceptance is not an issue. But then she read a small article about the ACLU's third lawsuit against James DeWeese, a judge of the Richland County Court of Common Pleas, who displayed the Ten Commandments in his courtroom.[25] "I have never been involved in the legal system, not even a traffic violation, so it never occurred to me that if I needed it that it might be biased against me simply due to my sexuality. Call me naïve. When I learned that he supported the Bible as the basis for laws in this country, it really struck me that many on the right use the Bible to deny my right to be a parent and even my existence as a lesbian. Would I find fair treatment in his court even for a case that has nothing to do with my sexuality?"

A 1997 report by the Lesbian and Gay Law Association of Greater New York (LeGaL) found that 56 percent of respondents witnessed bias-related incidents in courts, including "'gay-bashing' remarks," "gay jokes," "express references to 'homos,'" and "'gay male' mimicry of the limp wrist genre."[26] A 1998 study of the New Jersey state court system found that 79 percent of gay and lesbian respondents reported witnessing offensive gestures, disparaging remarks, and offensive jokes.[27] And for LGBTs arrested for a crime, the quality of representation they receive is often inadequate, particularly if they are poor or working-class. According to Abbe Smith, a former Philadelphia public defender, queer criminal defendants "are notoriously badly treated throughout the criminal justice system; police are nasty to them . . . court personnel often mock them; it is the rare judge or magistrate who treats these defendants with dignity or respect."[28]

Intimate Partner Violence

Irene stolidly detailed the years of physical abuse that had occurred at the hands of her now deceased partner, Dede. She had obviously told this story many times before throughout her years of volunteer work in women's shelters: "I loved her very much, and I still miss her all these years later. But she did abuse me, and she abused my daughter from my marriage. When she had been drinking and frustrated with her job, we would be on the receiving end of her fury. I finally told her I was leaving and taking my daughter with me. It was an ultimatum, drinking or her family. She couldn't have both. And, thank god, she chose us. Through the rest of our eight years together she lapsed two times, and she never abused us again."

I asked her whether she had ever felt fearful for her life.

"Of course. Look at me . . . I'm not the butch type. Dede was. I'm sorry to use stereotypes, but I'm old-fashioned, and the butch/femme roles were part of our upbringings. When Dede was mad and drunk, she aimed to hurt. And she did. This was overt, no-holds-barred physical abuse."

I asked if she had ever contacted the police, and this question elicited the first evidence of emotion since our conversation began. Was it amusement? Incredulousness? Possibly even scorn? I began to silently question if I had somehow inadvertently insulted her. After a few moments of awkward silence, she finally responded: "Of course I didn't. Can you imagine a lesbian living in rural Minnesota contacting the sheriff's office about domestic violence being perpetrated *by another woman?* That would have only made our situation worse. Far worse."

Though Irene's experiences of domestic violence occurred more than twenty-five years ago, her thoughts about police involvement still resonate.

The National Center for Victims of Crime estimates that intimate partner violence occurs in the relationships of LGBT people at about the same rate as in heterosexual relationships, or in approximately 25 to 33 percent of all relationships.[29] Its *National Survey of Violence Against Women* reported that slightly more than 11 percent of the women who had lived with a woman as part of a couple reported being raped, physically assaulted, and/or stalked by a female cohabitant.[30] In another study, 39 percent of gay men reported at least one type of physical abuse by a partner over a five-year period.[31] Finally, the NCAVP has been tracking LGBT intimate partner violence since 1998 and found a 15 percent increase since 2008.[32] Yet, as with hate crimes, LGBT victims of partner violence often do not report this violence.[33]

Victims of partner violence hesitate to contact law enforcement for many of the same reasons they decline to seek assistance for other forms of violence. They also fear being arrested themselves, worry about how their partner would be treated in police custody because of his or her LGBT identity, and are concerned that reporting this violence will out them to the community, thus having repercussions for their careers and relationships with family and friends. Finally, LGBT victims of domestic violence may hesitate to disclose partner violence for fear that the abuse will be considered evidence that the victim's sexual orientation and/or gender identity is unhealthy and is to blame for the abuse.

Accessing Help

In 2010 the National Center for Victims of Crime and the NCAVP surveyed community-based organizations and victim-assistance providers regarding their work with LGBT victims and survivors of violence. The results were not encouraging. Among the findings:[34]

- There is a dearth of culturally competent victim services for LGBT victims of crime.
- Victim-serving agencies are not well trained to work with LGBT victims and survivors of crime.
- LGBT victims of crime encounter homophobia, biphobia, transphobia, and heterosexism in their efforts to secure assistance.
- Of the few victim-support programs supporting LGBTs, most are small, staffed largely by volunteers, underfunded, and lack the capacity to engage in the outreach, education, and advocacy. Additionally, these programs are often understaffed.
- Few national violence prevention or intervention organizations highlight the needs of LGBT victims.

These findings are particularly discouraging, since the psychological outcomes of hate-crime victimization tend to be pernicious. Recent hate-crime victimization appears to be associated with greater psychological distress for gay men and lesbians than is victimization in non–hate crimes. In a well-received and often-cited study, lesbians and gay men who had experienced an assault or other person crime based on their sexual orientation within the previous five years reported significantly more symptoms of depression, traumatic stress, anxiety, and anger those who experienced non-bias crimes. Also, gay and lesbian victims of hate crimes were more likely than other respondents to regard the world as unsafe, people as malevolent, and report feelings of vulnerability and powerlessness.[35]

There are also few community supports for LGBTs experiencing domestic violence. Consider the case of Deborah, a lesbian woman in her thirties who sought help for domestic violence:

My partner, two children, and I are experiencing domestic violence from my ex-husband. I've been trying to find a way that we can all stay together and be safe, but am having a lot of trouble. Both of my kids have been molested, and one now has a teddy bear with GPS recording, just to be safe. My ex-husband is filing for temporary custody, so I'm not sure what I have to do legally to keep them safest with me. I got a protection order against my ex, but my partner has been denied. I don't understand why, because she's in danger too. When we tried to get into a confidential shelter, we were denied because they won't let couples in. I tried to explain that my partner has a disability and that I'm her caretaker, so we can't be separated. It didn't make any difference.[36]

At the societal level, the queer community has been disinclined to confront the amount of domestic violence in LGBT relationships, recognizing that such details would only detract from the image they are carefully crafting to make such unions more palatable. According to Joey Mogul, Andrea Ritchie, and Kay Whitlock, both policymakers and traditional service providers elide LGBT domestic violence so as not to appear to be condoning these relationships.[37]

Remedies

For the foreseeable future, LGBTs and their families will no doubt continue to be targeted for societal antipathy and harassment and occasional violence in their local communities. The backlash of inflammatory and hate-filled rhetoric inviting violence has increased as courts and the legislative systems belatedly acknowledge the fundamental human rights of LGBTs.

Few people voluntarily seek the status of a social pariah, and LGBT parents are particularly worried that disclosure of their same-sex interest will result in social ostracism—and worse—for themselves and even their children. Community members may be generally uninformed about LGBTs, and their knowledge base is built on stereotypes, misconceptions, and outright lies. For example, several parents informed me that a brief visit by the Capturing Momentum Tour, a ninety-nine-county "educational" trek by Bob Vander Plaats of the Iowa Family Leader (a "family values" organization) raised community hackles sufficiently enough to warrant maintaining a low profile and continued secrecy. They weren't about to out themselves before this visit, but the brief community "dialogue" instigated by the tour only supported the wisdom of their decision.

The tour originated after Iowa conservatives successfully ousted three Iowa Supreme Court justices who had voted in favor of marriage equality, and it set up discussions in small towns across the state in pizza parlors, coffee houses, small businesses, and an occasional City Hall. At one stop, Vander Plaats warned that homosexuality was a public health risk: "If we're teaching the kids, 'Don't smoke, because that's a risky health style,' the same can be true of the homosexual lifestyle."[38]

If their neighbors believe that specific health consequences associated with homosexuality (e.g., sexual minorities are overrepresented in their need for mental-health and drug and alcohol treatment services or the statistics regarding gay men and sexually transmitted diseases) are actually *caused by* homosexuality, then LGBT families are unlikely to be given a warm welcome. Those who look at the facts understand that these consequences are the result of societal stigma, homonegativity, and internalized homophobia and heterosexism, but this is a tough sell for neighbors when well-known figures are promulgating untrue, derogatory information. To these individuals, gay men and women are threats to their own families as well as the community at large.

For out LGBT families, particularly those in middle- and upper-income brackets, there are interventions for hate crimes, violence, and discrimination. For example, BiasHELP, a Long Island agency dedicated to prevention of bias crimes, hate-related harassment, bullying, and discrimination, recommends that victims call 911 if there is an immediate threat, document the incident(s), talk to a trustworthy person for support, consider reporting threats or acts of violence to the police, and obtain counseling for psychological repercussions.[39] But for less-out (and completely closeted) families and those who have reasons to be doubtful of the involvement of the police, there are fewer interventions and solutions, a concern noted by several prominent social justice organizations.

The NCAVP, for example, offered a series of recommendations to increase the responsiveness of the legal system to LGBT concerns, such as augmenting funding for LGBT services, expanding these services, and educating law enforcement officials and victim-services providers about LGBT issues and needs, but it also recognizes that if and when these changes occur, a great many LGBT families and individuals will still not seek the involvement of the legal system; police involvement works best for particular subset of the LGBT community (and rarely for transgender individuals) but, for the majority, is to be avoided. Thus, the NCAVP reports, "A small but growing number of organizations are developing skills and best practices on anti-violence work separate from the criminal legal system. These . . . promising strategies aim to strengthen local community ties between neighbors, local businesses, and community organizations. These strategies involve training participants in how to identify, de-escalate anti-LGBTQH violence, and support survivors without relying upon law enforcement."[40] One frequently cited example is the S.O.S. Collective of the Audre Lorde Project, which recruited restaurants, schools, churches, and other community organizations to become "safe spaces" for LGBT people of color.

In 2009 several national LGBT organizations declined to support the passage of the Matthew Shepard and James Byrd, Jr. Hate Crimes Prevention Act, including the Sylvia Rivera Law Project (SRLP), FIERCE, the Transformative Justice Law Project, the Transgender Intersex Justice Project, Right Rides, and Queers for Economic Justice. According to SRLP, "The recent expansion of the federal hate crimes legislation has received extensive praise and celebration by mainstream lesbian, gay, bisexual and transgender organizations because it purports to 'protect' LGBT people from attacks on the basis of their expressed and/or perceived identities for the first time ever on a federal level. . . . The evidence also shows that hate crime laws and other 'get tough on crime' measures do not deter or prevent violence. Increased incarceration does not deter others from committing violent acts motivated by hate, does not rehabilitate those who have committed past acts of hate, and does not make anyone safer."[41]

✦ ✦ ✦

According to Sharon Stapel of the New York Anti-Violence Project, "There is no one panacea for the many problems confronting LGBTQ populations . . . working with the police is not the only way—and sometimes not even the best way—to solve our problems."[42] But for now, this leaves many LGBT families in a state of limbo, unsure of how to handle threats to their existence. Maintaining a low profile and hunkering down as a family will only go so far. Obviously there is a long way to go, and much change is needed at the community level.

Conclusion

In *Seeing Like a State: How Certain Schemes to Improve the Human Condition Have Failed*, James Scott, professor of both political science and anthropology at Yale University, critiques current urban planning models and strongly supports the power of diversity: "Like the diverse old-growth forest, a richly differentiated neighborhood . . . is virtually, by definition, a more resilient and durable neighborhood. . . . Like monocropped forests, single-purpose districts, although they may initially catch a boom, are especially susceptible to stress. The diverse neighborhood is sustainable."[1]

Is this merely a utopian dream? Scott Page, a professor of economics and political science at the University of Michigan, analyzed the data regarding diversity to see if such claims were justified. He found that "the benefits of diversity do exist. They're not huge. We shouldn't expect them to be huge. But they're real, and over time, if we can leverage them, we'll be far better off. We'll find better solutions to our problems. We'll make better predictions. We'll live in a better place."[2]

Communities are indeed becoming more diverse. Communities are belatedly recognizing the presence of LGBTs living within their limits and that some of them have children. Additionally, traditional LGBT communities are evolving as they belatedly acknowledge parents in their midst, a group whose presence has too often been elided or marginalized. Communities that adapt—and, yes, struggle—with these changes will, in the end, be healthier and more resilient. Nonetheless, before we can reach this better place we must go through the struggles necessary for such growth—for while the outcomes of diversity are positive, the process of getting there is fraught with conflict.

Recommendations

On October 25, 2001, the report *All Children Matter*, a joint effort by the Movement Advancement Project, Family Equality Council, Center for American Progress, COLAGE, the Evan B. Donaldson Adoption Institute, and the National Association of Social Workers, was released. It details how archaic and discriminatory laws, combined with social stigma, have deleterious impacts on LGBT families, particularly their economic security, health and well-being, and ability to create stable, loving households. The document concludes with twenty pages of recommendations that, if implemented, would forever and positively impact the trajectory of LGBT parenting in the country. It has been justifiably lauded as the most exhaustive policy statement of LGBT families ever released.

The recommendations are broadly summarized into the following three categories:[3]

1. Allowing all children to create legal bonds with parents, regardless of their parents' sexual orientation, gender identity, or marital status. The need for comprehensive parental recognition laws at the state level to fully protect children in LGBT families is essential, and this encompasses passing or amending state adoption laws or regulations to allow unmarried and same-sex couples to jointly adopt and foster children. State laws should also allow those who show they have functioned as parents to seek not only custody and visitation rights but full parentage so that they may enjoy appropriate legal standing in the lives of children with whom they have formed a relationship, whether or not they have a biological or legal relationship to the children.

Also, binational same-sex couples should be able to sponsor a foreign national partner or spouse for immigration so that families are not under the threat of being torn apart when one parent cannot become a permanent resident or citizen. Other immigration laws impacting LGBT families were likewise targeted for reform.

2. Changing law and public policy to provide diverse families with equal access to government-based economic protections and programs. In her 2008 book *Beyond (Straight and Gay) Marriage*, Nancy Polikoff writes, "Laws that value all families . . . are about ensuring that every relationship and every family has the legal framework for economic and emotional security. Laws that value all families value same-sex couples but not only same-sex couples. Lesbian, gay, bisexual, and transgender people live in varied households and families. A valuing-all-families approach strives to meet then needs of all of them."[4] Similarly, *All Children Matter* recommends the implementation of a "consistent and broad definition of family across federal government programs [so that] diverse families would no longer have to navigate a maze of definitions (which results in some families being accurately included in some programs but not in others)."[5] Such programs include Temporary Assistance for Needy Families (TANF), food and nutrition assistance, public housing and housing assistance, Medicaid and the Children's Health Insurance Program (CHIP), Supplementary Social Security (SSI); education loans, grants, and scholarships, inheritance laws, wrongful death suits, and Social Security Survivors and Disability Insurance Benefits. The report also questions the US tax code, since it does not allow LGBT families to claim the deductions and credits available to married couples.

3. Actively creating a culture that affirms the value of all children and decreases stigma and discrimination against LGBT and other twenty-first-century families. It is this recommendation that is most relevant to the topic of this book—LGBT families coping with unwelcoming and intolerant communities. *All Children Matter* lists several pertinent goals, which, if achieved, would benefit all LGBT families regardless of their location:

> *Create a foundation of legal protections:* As noted earlier, the Matthew Shepard and James Byrd, Jr. Hate Crimes Prevention Act is a source of contention in LGBT communities, but, as it is, the Act authorizes the Department of Justice to investigate

and prosecute certain bias-motivated crimes based on the victim's actual or perceived sexual orientation, gender, or gender identity. For many in the LGBT communities, this was a giant leap forward.

However, other significant legal efforts have stalled. The Employment Non-Discrimination Act, for example, has been introduced into every Congress since 1994 but has yet to pass. It would prohibit discrimination against employees on the basis of sexual orientation or gender identity by civilian, nonreligious employers of fifteen or more employees. And while the Department of Housing and Urban Development (HUD) added new rules in 2011 banning discrimination against LGBT people by housing owners who receive HUD financing or housing that is insured by HUD, non-HUD entities remain exempt. Thus, in 2011, Senator John Kerry introduced the Housing Opportunities Made Equal Act (HOME Act), which bans discrimination on the basis of sexual orientation and gender identity in all housing as well as amend the Equal Credit Opportunity Act to prevent such discrimination in lending. "It's hard to believe that in 2011, any law-abiding, tax-paying American who can pay the rent can't live somewhere just because of who they are," Kerry said in a statement. "Housing discrimination against LGBT Americans is wrong, but today in most states there isn't a thing you can do about it."[6]

Finally, federal and state legislation should continue to address comprehensive school safety plans, including passing legislation that enumerates sexual orientation and gender identity as protected categories, and explicitly protect students from bullying and harassment based on their association with LGBT people to help ensure the safety of children with LGBT parents or friends.

Educate professionals: Efforts at eradicating discrimination necessitate educating professionals who come in contact with LGBT families regarding their issues and needs, including medical and mental health treatment providers, government agencies, the legal system, school personnel, and communities of faith.

Create organizations that welcome nontraditional families: Organizations and agencies that work with the public should adopt nondiscrimination policies that include family status, sexual orientation, and gender identity. LGBT families entering these premises should know that they are not merely acknowledged but also welcome.

Educate the public: The archetype of the traditional family headed by married different-sex parents is increasingly a relic of the past. Other family configurations now dominate, including single parents, children being raised by grandparents, blended families of divorce, two voluntarily unmarried cohabiting adults raising children, foster parents, and, of course, LGBT families. The public should be educated as to the true diversity of today's families in order to challenge the belief that they are of a secondary status in comparison to traditional family composition. Advocates should work to increase positive representations of LGBT families in the media and popular culture. We also need to depict the true diversity occurring *within* the broad category of LGBT families, particularly low-income families, rural families, families of color, and blended LGBT families where one parent is an acting or legal stepparent—not the stereotype of wealthy, urban, and white LGBTs that currently dominate the media.

Continue to cultivate allies: Allies are needed at the national and local levels. Being an ally requires a mind-set embracing openness, awareness of one's assumptions, confronting one's own prejudices, and believing in the dignity of all people. Being an ally also necessitates a set of behaviors such as standing up for the LGBT community, being inclusive, challenging hurtful and negative comments, and defending against discrimination.[7] As some of the narratives in this book indicate, straight allies are a treasured resource for LGBT families, particularly those who can't yet be out in their communities.

Offer resources for LGBT families: We can help LGBT families by educating them about laws and how to protect themselves, being allies, and providing opportunities for children with LGBT parents to interact, find support, and socialize.

Support research on LGBT families: We need more research on LGBT families. The question "Are children growing up in lesbian families or having gay fathers more at risk for psychological problems than other children?" has been answered. It is now time move forward and explore the myriad other challenges faced by the diverse demographic that comprises LGBT families.

Help those struggling with internalized homophobia and heterosexism: Fortunately, the social stigmatization of LGBTs is indeed decreasing and this seems to be having an impact on the composition of LGBT families. In the 2000 US Census, nearly 10 percent of same-sex, unmarried-partner couples raising children were in households with *an adopted child* present. Eight years later, data suggest that this had nearly doubled, to 19 percent. Yet this increase was offset by a decline in the number of LGBT parents giving birth to children within different-sex relationships, typically occurring when these individuals were young and less open about their sexual orientation.[8] According to a 2011 review of the topic, "Declines in social stigma toward LGBT people mean that more are coming out earlier in life and are becoming less likely to have children with different-sex partners. These declines may be outpacing increases in adoptive parenting and parenting using reproductive technologies."[9] Still, some LGBT parents may need professional help to deal with the suffocating shame that breeds within their own internalized homophobia and heterosexism.

I asked Jennifer Chrisler, executive director of the Family Equality Council—one of the most influential organizations in regard to LGBT families—for her perspective on what is necessary for the safety of LGBT families. Her response:

> The LGBT family movement is at an important point in history. Thirty years ago, the Family Equality Council was founded to fit the needs of a small group of newly divorced dads who had come out as gay and who were seeking to maintain contact with their biological children. Since that time, LGBT families have become more numerous and more visible and their needs have changed. Although great progress has been made in meeting those needs, there is considerable work to be done to ensure these families have adequate legal and economic protections. That is especially true for those families who live in communities where they are isolated or feel unwelcome.[10]

Chrisler also offered several key recommendations to make those communities and indeed our entire country a safer place for those families. These include:

- Engaging LGBT and straight allies in doing more to make these places more hospitable. We need multiple voices to make positive change and the loved ones and friends of LGBT families can have a huge impact.
- Leveraging the rising tide of change in states that are more progressive to help make incremental changes in the tougher states.
- Bringing more attention and investing more time to making positive policy changes in those states—so that the climate gets better.
- Focusing our advocacy work on issues that matter to low-income families to make sure we include broad definitions that help closeted LGBT families (e.g., access to early childcare programs, food stamps, health care).

- Creating a national dialogue about the diversity of our families and where they are living so that there is help coming from other places when these families are limited in their own ability to make change or stand up for their families.

The Long Road Ahead

Ironically, exactly one week after the release of the groundbreaking *All Families Matter* report, the US House of Representatives passed a resolution reaffirming "In God We Trust" as the country's motto. According to the *Washington Post*, "The deeper meaning behind this debate—saying it was a chance for the House to reassert that it believes there is divine goodness and order in the universe."[11] Not surprisingly, the resolution was approved by a 396–9 tally and "[m]any lawmakers threw their heart into the debate."[12] Others, however, saw through the smokescreen surrounding the vote; it was yet another attempt to reignite the "culture wars"—and, as this book has detailed, LGBT families are targets in these wars. Some of the underlying beliefs responsible for this backlash include: sexual minorities are pushing too hard for acceptance; sexual minorities are pushing for inclusion into places where they are not welcome; and social policies supporting the advancement of sexual minorities are ultimately unfair to heterosexuals. These are very same arguments that have been made to block gains by all minority groups, particularly people of color, and they are continually trotted out when a new demographic begins to make headway. It doesn't matter that research has unimpeachably demonstrated that LGBT parents are just as competent as heterosexual parents and the outcomes for their children are positive. A tenacious, well-organized, well-funded, and well-connected minority continues to excoriate these families and vehemently fight their progress.

LGBT families and their allies do not have the financial and political muscle of their detractors, and their successes have often come on the coattails of progress for LGBTs in general. For example, the repeated calls for more research regarding the medical and mental health needs of LGBTs inevitably advance our knowledge of LGBT parents. Efforts to increase the inclusiveness of religious institutions regarding LGBTs no doubt make these venues more approachable for LGBT families. Finally, the ongoing efforts at bullying prevention and intervention for all students cannot help but remedy the negative experiences encountered by children of LGBT parents. As acceptance of LGBTs grows, so too will the acceptance of LGBT parents and families, yet we have a long way to go. Progress is indeed being made, but skirmishes and occasional battles await LGBT families at the national, state, and, of most concern to many of these families, the local level before we have created thriving communities embracing the diversity of sexual orientation.

Notes

Unattributed quotes come from personal interviews conducted in 2011 with families around the country. To maintain their privacy, full names have not been given and, in some cases, pseudonyms have been used.

Introduction

1. Eileen Chamberlain Donahoe, statement to the UN Human Rights Council, March 22, 2011.
2. Jon W. Davidson, "Transforming Hearts and Minds," *Impact* 28, no. 3 (2011): 19.
3. In December 2010 the US State Department announced a redesign of the Consular Report of Birth Abroad (an application for US citizenship for a child born overseas to a US citizen) and the DS-11 Passport Application (required for first-time passport applicants and applicants who are under sixteen years of age). The new forms request information about "Mother/Parent 1" and "Father/ Parent 2" to allow a gender-neutral description of a child's parents.
4. Institute of Medicine [US] Committee on Lesbian, Gay, Bisexual, and Transgender Health Issues and Research Gaps and Opportunities, *The Health of Lesbian, Gay, Bisexual, and Transgender People: Building a Foundation for Better Understanding* (Washington, DC: National Academies Press, 2011).
5. Cited in Rob Boston, "Religious Right Rebound," *Church & State* 64, no. 5 (2011): 7.
6. Gallup Organization, "Values and Beliefs" survey, administered between May 5 and 8, 2011. Support for the moral acceptability of gay and lesbian relations reaches 64 percent.
7. Michelangelo Signorile, "The Bully Pulpit," *Advocate*, December 2010.
8. Ibid.
9. Joe Solmonese, "Letter from the President: Pushing Toward the Tipping Point for Equality," *Equality*, Fall 2011, 2.
10. "DOMA Doubts," *Advocate*, May 2011, 10.
11. Michelle Cretella, "Homosexual Parenting: Is It Time For Change?" American College of Pediatricians, http://www.acpeds.org/.
12. Jeff Buchanan, "What Does Exodus Believe About Same-Sex Parenting and Adoption?" Exodus International, http://exodusinternational.org/.
13. Sabrina Tavernise, "Adoptions by Gay Couples Rise, Despite Barriers," *New York Times*, January 13, 2011, http://www.nytimes.com/.

14. Fintan Moore, Vicki Wunsch, and Barbara Satin, *All in God's Family: Creating Allies for Our LGBT Families* (Minneapolis: National Gay and Lesbian Task Force's Institute for Welcoming Resources), 3.
15. Theodore B. Olson, "The Conservative Case for Gay Marriage," *Newsweek*, January 18, 2010, 52.
16. "Poll Finds Most in US Back Gay Marriage," *Boston Globe*, March 19, 2011, http://www.boston.com/.

Chapter 1: The Diversity of LGBT Parents

1. Sabrina Tavernise, "Parenting by Gays More Common in the South, Census Shows," *New York Times*, January 18, 2011, www.nytimes.com/.
2. Ibid.
3. Ibid.
4. Fiona Tasker and Charlotte Patterson, "Research on Gay and Lesbian Parenting: Retrospect and Prospect," *Journal of GLBT Family Studies* 3, nos. 2–3 (2007): 25.
5. Randy Albelda et al., *Poverty in the Lesbian, Gay, and Bisexual Community* (Los Angeles: Williams Institute, 2009).
6. Adam Romero, Amanda Baumle, M. V. Lee Badgett, and Gary Gates, *Census Snapshot 2007* (Los Angeles: Williams Institute, 2007), http://www.escholarship.org.
7. Albelda et al., *Poverty in the Lesbian, Gay, and Bisexual Community*.
8. Jon Binnie, *The Globalization of Sexuality* (London: Sage Publications, 2004).
9. Ramona Faith Oswald and Linda S. Culton, "Under the Rainbow: Rural Gay Life and Its Relevance for Family Providers," *Family Relations* 52, no. 1 (2003).
10. Ibid.
11. Bianca D. M. Wilson, *Our Families: Attributes of Bay Area Lesbian, Gay, Bisexual & Transgender Parents and Their Children* (San Francisco: Our Family Coalition, 2007).
12. Craig J. Konnoth and Gary J. Gates, *Same-Sex Couples and Immigration in the United States*, (Los Angeles: Williams Institute, 2011), http://williamsinstitute.law.ucla.edu.
13. Timothy J. Biblarz and Evren Savci, "Lesbian, Gay, Bisexual and Transgender Families," *Journal of Marriage and Family* 72 (June 2010).
14. Quoted in Jen Colletta, "Census: 33K Gay Couples in PA, 19 Percent in Philly," *Philadelphia Gay News*, July 1, 2011.
15. Straight Spouse Network, http://www.straightspouse.org/.
16. Personal communication, July 1, 2011.
17. Dana Rudolph, "Double the Pregnancies, Double the Fun," *Philadelphia Gay News*, April 1, 2011.

Chapter 2: The War on LGBT Families

1. Presidential Proclamation—Lesbian, Gay, Bisexual, and Transgender Pride Month, May 31, 2011, http://www.whitehouse.gov/.
2. D'Anne Witkowski, "Creep of the Week: Sally Kern," *Philadelphia Gay News*, http://epgn.com.

3. Ian Thompson, "NOM Marriage Pledge: A Discriminatory, Tone-Deaf Pitfall," American Civil Liberties Union, http://www.aclu.org.

4. Quoted by D'Anne Witkowski, "Creep of the Week: Pat Robertson," *Philadelphia Gay News*, http://epgn.com.

5. National Coalition of Anti-Violence Programs, *Annual Report on Anti-LGBT Hate Violence Released*, May 20, 2008, http://www.ncavp.org/.

6. Muzafer Sherif, *In Common Predicament: Social Psychology of Intergroup Conflict and Cooperation* (Boston: Houghton Mifflin, 1966).

7. Philip Zimbardo, *The Lucifer Effect* (New York: Random House, 2008).

8. Aaron T. Beck, *Prisoners of Hate* (New York: Harper Collins, 1999), 153.

9. Evelyn Schlatter and Robert Steinback, "10 Myths," *Southern Poverty Law Center Intelligence Report* 140 (2010): 33.

10. Greenberg Quinlan Rosner Research, "HRC Frequency Questionnaire," administered July 16–19, 2011.

11. Ibid.

12. See, for example, Susan Golombok, "Foreword: Research on Gay and Lesbian Parenting: An Historical Perspective Across 30 Years," *Journal of GLBT Family Studies* 3, nos. 2–3 (2007).

13. Bottoms v. Bottoms, 457 S.E.2d 102 (Va. 1995).

14. Gary Stein, "Child Custody Ruling Lacks Understanding," SunSentinel.com, February 4, 1996, http://articles.sun-sentinel.com; Brief for Andrew E. Cherlin et al. as amici curiae supporting appellees Baehr v. Miike, No. 91–139405, 1996, WL 694235 (Hawaii Cir. Ct. December 3, 1996).

15. Cynthia Yockey, "Equality Will Come From the Right," *Advocate*, October 2011, 51.

16. Traditional Values Coalition, "Traditional Values Explained," http://www.traditionalvalues.org/

17. Quoted in Sue E. Spivey and Christine M. Robinson, "Genocidal Intentions: Social Death and the Ex-Gay Movement," *Genocide Intentions and Prevention* 5, no.1 (2010): 79.

18. Evelyn Schlatter, "The Hard Liners," *Southern Poverty Law Center Intelligence Report* 140 (2010): 35.

19. Schlatter and Steinback, "10 Myths"; Spivey and Robinson, "Genocidal Intentions."

20. Jason Childs, "Conversion Story: A Former Jerry Falwell Follower Reflects on How the Religious Right Gets It Wrong," *Church & State* 64, no. 5 (2011): 21.

21. Cited in Spivey and Robinson, "Genocidal Intentions."

22. Ibid.

23. Julie Harren, "To Educate the Public on the Issue of Homosexuality," presentation at the Exodus Freedom Conference, Ridgecrest, NC, July 2005.

24. Luisita Lopez Torregrosa, "Gay Torture in New York: Gang of Nine Accused," PoliticsDaily.com, September 10, 2010, http://www.politicsdaily.com/.

25. Mark Potok, "Under Attack," *Southern Poverty Law Center Intelligence Report* 140 (2010).

26. NCAVP, *Hate Violence Against Lesbian, Gay, Bisexual, Transgender, Queer and HIV-Affected Communities in the United States in 2010* (New York: National Coalition of Anti-Violence Programs, 2011).

27. American Psychological Association, "Hate Crimes Today: An Age-Old Foe In Modern Dress," APA Position Papers (1998): 1.

28. Cited in Potok, "Under Attack," 28.

29. Gary J. Gates, M.V. Lee Badgett, Kate Chambers, and Jennifer Macomber, *Adoption and Foster Care by Gay and Lesbian Parents in the United States (2007)*, report by the Williams Institute and the Urban Institute, http://www.law.ucla.edu/.

30. Sabrina Tavernise, "Adoptions by Gay Couples Rise, Despite Barriers," *New York Times*, June 13, 2011, http://www.nytimes.com/.

31. Ibid.

32. Gates et al., *Adoption and Foster Care*.

33. Committee on Psychosocial Aspects of Child and Family Health, "Coparent or Second-Parent Adoption by Same-Sex Parents," *Pediatrics* 109, no. 2 (2002).

34. Michelle Cretella, "Homosexual Parenting: Is It Time for Change?" American College of Pediatricians, http://www.acpeds.org/.

35. See "Catholic Charities Drops Ill. Foster Care Lawsuit," Americans United bulletin, January 2012, http://www.au.org/.

Chapter 3: Passing

1. Richard Florida, "Top Metros for Same-Sex Couples with Children," Alantic.com, June 28, 2011, http://www.theatlantic.com/.

2. Sharon S. Rostosky, "Marriage Amendments and Psychological Distress in Lesbian, Gay, and Bisexual Adults," *Journal of Counseling Psychology* 56, no. 56 (2009): 56–66.

3. Nathaniel M. Lewis, "Mental Health in Sexual Minorities: Recent Indicators, Trends, and Their Relationships to Place in North America and Europe," *Health & Place* 15, no. 4 (2009).

4. Abbie E. Goldberg and JuliAnna Z. Smith, "Stigma, Social Context, and Mental Health: Lesbian and Gay Couples Across the Transition to Adoptive Parenthood," *Journal of Counseling Psychology* 58, no. 1 (2011).

5. David Crary, "Most States Likely to Spurn Gay-Marriage Bandwagon," Associated Press, July 25, 2011.

6. Ibid.

7. Human Rights Campaign, "Landscape of On the Road to Equality Tour States," August 2011, http://www.hrc.org/.

8. Sean G. Massey, "Sexism, Heterosexism, and Attributions About Undesirable Behavior in Children of Gay, Lesbian, and Heterosexual Parents," *Journal of GLBT Family Studies* 3, no. 4 (2007): 458.

9. Joe Kort, *Gay Affirmative Therapy for the Straight Clinician* (New York: Norton, 2008).

10. Bianca D. M. Wilson, *Our Families: Attributes of Bay Area Lesbian, Gay, Bisexual & Transgender Parents and Their Children* (San Francisco: Our Family Coalition, 2007): 4.

11. Craig Fuller, Doris Chang, and Lisa Rubin, "Sliding Under the Radar: Passing and Power Among Sexual Minorities," *Journal of LGBT Issues in Counseling* 3 (2009).

12. Abigail Garner, *Families Like Mine: Children of Gay Parents Tell It Like It Is* (New York: Perennial Currents, 2004), 37.

Chapter 4: The Stress of the Ideal Family

1. Matthew Hoffman, "Exclusive Interview with Lisa Miller, Ex-Lesbian Fighting for Custody of Own Child," LifeSiteNews.com, http://www.lifesitenews.com/.

2. Ibid.

3. Caitlin Ryan, *Supportive Families, Healthy Children: Helping Families with Lesbian, Gay, Bisexual & Transgender Children* (San Francisco: Family Acceptance Project, Marian Wright Edelman Institute, San Francisco State University, 2009). Reprinted with permission.

4. Joe Kort, *Gay Affirmative Therapy for the Straight Clinician* (New York: Norton, 2008).

5. Joseph Neisen, "Healing from Cultural Victimization: Recovery from Shame Due to Heterosexism," *Journal of Gay and Lesbian Psychotherapy* 2, no. 1 (1993).

6. Don Wright, "Illusions of Intimacy," in *Gay Men and Childhood Sexual Trauma: Integrating the Shattered Self*, ed. J. Cassese (New York: Harrington Park, 2000).

7. Personal communication, June 20, 2011.

8. Fred Fejes, *Gay Rights and Moral Panic* (New York: Palgrave Macmillan, 2008), 137–38.

9. Sabrina Tavernise, "Adoptions by Gay Couples Rise, Despite Barriers," *New York Times*, June 13, 2011, www.nytimes.com/.

10. Sue Hyde, *Come Out and Win* (Boston: Beacon Press, 2007), 55.

11. Abigail Garner, *Families Like Mine: Children of Gay Parents Tell It Like It Is* (New York: Perennial Currents, 2004), 37.

12. Timothy Biblarz and Evren Savci, "Lesbian, Gays, Bisexual, and Transgender Families," *Journal of Marriage and Family* 72 (June 2010): 492.

13. Joanna Bunker Rohrbaugh, "Lesbian Families: Clinical Issues and Theoretical Implications," *Professional Psychology: Research and Practice* 23, no. 6 (1992).

14. Tian Dayton, "The Set Up: Living with Addiction," National Association for Children of Alcoholics, http://www.tiandayton.com/.

15. "Talking to Children About Our Families," Family Equality Council, http://www.familyequality.org.

16. COLAGE, "Coming Out To Your Kids," http://www.colage.org/.

17. Dana G. Finnegan and Emily B. McNally, *Counseling Lesbian, Gay, Bisexual, and Transgender Substance Abusers* (New York: Haworth Press, 2002), 179.

18. Sandra Anderson, *Substance Abuse Disorders in Lesbian, Gay, Bisexual, & Transgender Clients* (New York: Columbia University Press, 2009), 85.

19. Joe Kort, *Gay Affirmative Therapy for the Straight Clinician* (New York: Norton, 2008), 138.

Chapter 5: Schools

1. Nick Wing and Clint McCance, "Arkansas School Board Member, Wants 'Fags' To Commit Suicide," *Huffington Post*, October 27, 2010, www.huffingtonpost.com/.

2. Will Kohler, "Anti-Gay N.J. Teacher Vickie Knox: Gov. Chris Christie Condemns and NOM and the ACLU Defends," Back2Stonewall, October 20 2011, http://www .back2stonewall.com/.

3. Ibid.

4. Alicia Crowl, Soyeon Ahn, and Jean Baker, "A Meta-Analysis of Developmental Outcomes for Children of Same-Sex and Heterosexual Parents," *Journal of GLBT Family Studies* 4, no. 3 (2008): 386.

5. Joseph G. Kosciw and Elizabeth M. Diaz, *Involved, Invisible, Ignored: The Experiences of Lesbian, Gay, Bisexual, and Transgender Parents and Their Children in Our Nation's K–12 Schools* (New York: Gay, Lesbian, and Straight Education Network, 2008).

6. Ibid., 66.

7. Ibid.

8. Ibid., 67.

9. Ibid.

10. Tina Fakhrid-Deen, *Let's Get This Straight* (Berkeley, CA: Seal Press, 2011), 99.

11. *All Children Matter: How Legal and Social Inequalities Hurt LGBT Families* (Denver: Movement Advancement Project/Family Equality Council/Center for American Progress, October 2011).

12. Ibid.

13. Kosciw and Diaz, *Involved, Invisible, Ignored*.

14. Council for American Private Education, "Facts and Studies," http://www.capenet .org/.

15. *All Children Matter*.

16. Virginia Casper, Steven Schultz, and Elaine Wickens, "Breaking the Silences: Lesbian and Gay Parents and the Schools," *Teachers College Record* 94, no. 1 (1992).

17. *All Children Matter*.

18. Ibid.

19. Kosciw and Diaz, *Involved, Invisible, Ignored*.

20. Ibid., 82.

21. Ibid., 81.

22. Ibid., 79.

23. Ibid., 80.

24. Ibid., 82.

25. Ibid., 82.

26. Ibid., 81.

27. Ibid., 82.

28. Enid Lee, "Taking Multicultural, Anti-Racist Education Seriously: An Interview with Enid Lee," in *Rethinking Multicultural Education*, ed. W. Au (Milwaukee: Rethinking Schools Publication, 2009), 11–13.

29. Stuart Biegel, "Teachable Moments," *Advocate*, April 2011, 20.

30. Ibid., 20.
31. Kosciw and Diaz, *Involved, Invisible, Ignored.*
32. Equality California, press release, December 13, 2010, http://www.eqca.org/.
33. Family Research Council, "Stop SB48-Protect Parental Rights," http://www.youtube.com/.
34. "Family Research Council's Repeal SB 48 Campaign Warns Chaz Bono Will Replace George Washington," *Huffington Post,* October 6, 2011, http://www.huffingtonpost.com/.
35. Dana Rudolph, "Where Are the LGBT Biographies for Kids?" *Philadelphia Gay News,* November 25, 2011.
36. Quoted in Ruth Fine, "California Schools Scramble to Implement LGBT Curriculum Before Deadline," *San Diego LGBT Weekly,* October 21, 2011, http://lgbtweekly.com/.
37. "Texas School Board Votes to Reject Creationist Materials," *Church & State* 64, no. 8 (2011): 18.
38. Sandhya Bathija, "From Creationism in Public Schools to Government Aid for Religion, Church-State Battles Are Erupting in Legislatures Across the Country," *Church & State* 64, no. 4 (2011).
39. Ibid.
40. Ibid.
41. Vicki Glembocki, "Toto, We're Not in the Gayborhood Anymore," *G Philly* (Fall 2011): 48.
42. "Missouri School District Censors 'Anti-Bible' Books," *Church & State* 64, no. 8 (2011): 3.
43. Robert P. Doyle, *Books Challenged or Banned in 2010–2011* (Chicago: American Library Association, 2011).
44. "*And Tango Makes Three* Waddles Its Way Back to the Number One Slot as America's Most Frequently Challenged Book," American Library Association, http://www.ala.org/.
45. Kosciw and Diaz, *Involved, Invisible, Ignored.*
46. Ibid.
47. Chris Hampton, "*Don't Filter Me!*" Interim Report, February 1–August 31, 2011, ACLU, http://www.aclu.org/.
48. Ibid.
49. "ACLU Targets Schools in PA as Part of National 'Don't Filter Me' LGBT Initiative," *Free for All* [publication of the ACLU of Pennsylvania] (Summer 2011).
50. Ibid.
51. Alexandra Rockey Fleming and Bob Meadows, "A School to Feel Safe," *People,* March 8, 2010, http://www.people.com/.
52. Kayla Webley, "A Separate Peace?" *Time,* October 24, 2011, 46.
53. Ibid., 44.
54. Gay, Lesbian, and Straight Education Network, "Background and Information About Gay-Straight Alliances," GLSEN, http://www.glsen.org/.
55. "About Gay-Straight Alliances," GLSEN, http://www.glsen.org/.

56. Russell B. Toomey, Caitlin Ryan, Rafael M. Diaz, and Stephen T. Russell, "High School Gay-Straight Alliances (GSAs) and Young Adult Well-Being: An Examination of GSA Presence, Participation, and Perceived Effectiveness," *Applied Developmental Science* 15, no. 4 (2011).

57. Ibid.

58. "Flour Bluff High School Acknowledges Gay-Straight Alliance Club Has the Right to Meet," American Civil Liberties Union, March 9, 2011, http://www.aclu.org/.

59. Kaitlin Mayhew, "Education Department to Study School Bullying Policies," *Youth Today*, June 20, 2011, http://youthtoday.org/.

60. US Department of Education, "Guidance Targeting Harassment Outlines Local and Federal Responsibility," October 26, 2010, http://www.ed.gov/.

61. US Department of Education, "Key Policy Letters from the Education Secretary and Deputy Secretary," December 16, 2010, http://www2.ed.gov/.

62. D'Anne Witkowski, "Creep of the Week: Michigan Republican State Senators," *Philadelphia Gay News*, November 11–17, 2011.

63. Ibid.

64. Ibid.

65. Kosciw and Diaz, *Involved, Invisible, Ignored*, xv.

Chapter 6: Professional Services

1. *When Health Care Isn't Caring: Lambda Legal's Survey of Discrimination Against LGBT People and People with HIV* (New York: Lambda Legal, 2010), http://www.lambdalegal.org/.

2. Chris Geidner, "Janice Langbehn Honored with Presidential Citizens Medal," *Metro-Weekly*, October 20, 2011, http://metroweekly.com/.

3. *Healthcare Equality Index 2011* (Washington, DC: Human Rights Campaign Foundation, 2011).

4. Juno Obedin-Maliver, Elizabeth S. Goldsmith, Leslie Stewart, et al., "Lesbian, Gay, Bisexual, and Transgender–Related Content in Undergraduate Medical Education," *Journal of the American Medical Association* 306, no. 9 (2011): 971–77.

5. Quoted in Tracie White, "Lesbian, Gay, Bisexual and Transgendered Health Issues Not Being Taught at Medical Schools, Study Finds," Stanford School of Medicine, September 6, 2011, http://med.stanford.edu/.

6. Todd Melby, "The Nation's LGBT Health Check-Up," *Contemporary Sexuality* 45, no. 8 (2011): 5.

7. Ibid.

8. *When Health Care Isn't Caring.*

9. Ibid.

10. Ibid.

11. "Facts About Patient-Centered Communications," Joint Commission, 2011, http://www.jointcommission.org.

12. Ibid.

13. Kellan Baker and Jeff Krehely, *Changing the Game: What Health Care Reform Means for Lesbian, Gay, Bisexual, and Transgender Americans* (Washington, DC: Center for American Progress, 2011): 26.

14. Joel Ginsberg, *Provisions Related to the Care of Lesbian, Gay, Bisexual, and Transgender (LGBT) Patients and Their Families* (San Francisco: Gay and Lesbian Medical Association, 2010), 1, 2.

15. IOM [Institute of Medicine], *The Health of Lesbian, Gay, Bisexual, and Transgender People: Building a Foundation for Better Understanding* (Washington, DC: The National Academies Press, 2011).

16. Melby, "The Nation's LGBT Health Check-Up."

17. "Administration Priorities," *Philadelphia Gay News*, March 17, 2012.

18. Melby, "The Nation's LGBT Health Check-Up."

19. National Alliance on Mental Illness, "Facts on Children's Mental Health in America," http://www.nami.org/.

20. Mental Health America, "Children's Mental Health Statistics," http://www.nmha.org/.

21. Ibid.

22. N. E. Whitehead, "Homosexuality and Mental Health Problems," National Association for Research and Therapy of Homosexuality, http://www.narth.com/.

23. Peter Sprigg, *The Top Ten Myths About Homosexuality* (Washington, DC: Family Research Council, 2010), 22. Available at http://www.frc.org/.

24. Ibid., 7.

25. Ibid., 30.

26. Just the Facts Coalition, *Just the Facts about Sexual Orientation & Youth: A Primer for Principals, Educators, and School Personnel* (Washington, DC: American Psychological Association, 2008), http://www.apa.org/.

27. Ibid., 5.

28. *When Health Care Isn't Caring.*

29. Jacky Coates and Richard Sullivan, "Achieving Competent Family Practice with Same-Sex Parents: Some Promising Directions," *Journal of GLBT Family Studies* 1, no. 2 (2005): 91.

30. "Medical Schools Devote Just Five Hours to LGBT Issues," *Contemporary Sexuality* 46, no. 1 (2012): 6.

31. "Defending Freedom, Statehouse by Statehouse," *Civil Liberties: The American Civil Liberties Union National Newspaper*, Summer 2011.

32. Sandhya Bathija, "Counseling Clash," *Church & State* 64, no. 4 (2011): 14.

33. Alliance Defense Fund, "The Work of the Alliance Defense Fund," http://www.alliancedefensefund.org/.

34. Sandhya Bathija, "Counseling Clash."

35. Ibid.

36. Center for Substance Abuse Treatment, *A Provider's Introduction to Substance Abuse Treatment for Lesbian, Gay, Bisexual, and Transgender Individuals* (Rockville, MD: US Department of Health and Human Services, 2001).

37. Joe Kort, *Gay Affirmative Therapy for the Straight Clinician* (New York: Norton, 2008), 19.

38. American Psychological Association, "Guidelines for Psychotherapy with Lesbian, Gay, & Bisexual Clients," *American Psychologist* 55 (2000).

39. Ibid.

40. *Healthcare Equality Index*, 14.

41. *When Health Care Isn't Caring.*

42. Marjorie E. Baker, "Cultural Differences in the Use of Advance Directives: A Review of the Literature," Research Center for Group Dynamics, University of Michigan, 2000, http://www.rcgd.isr.umich.edu/.

43. "Hospital Visitation," presidential memorandum, April 15, 2010, http://www.whitehouse .gov.

44. *Lifelines: Documents to Protect You and Your Family* (San Francisco: National Center for Lesbian Rights), http://www.nclrights.org.

45. Melby, "The Nation's LGBT Health Check-Up."

46. Ibid.

Chapter 7: Recreation and Leisure

1. Silver Dollar City website, http://www.bransonsilverdollarcity.com/.

2. American Camp Association website, "The Value of Camp," http://www.campparents .org/.

3. 4-H website, "Who We Are," http://www.4-h.org/.

4. Personal communication, December 5, 2011.

5. Fred Bernstein, "For Gay Parents, A Big Week in the Sun," *New York Times*, July 22, 2007, http://travel.nytimes.com/.

6. Ibid.

7. Nicole Zarrett and Richard M. Lerner, "Ways to Promote the Positive Development of Children and Youth," *Child Trends Research to Results Brief* (2007): 2.

8. Reed Larson, Jacquelynne Eccles, and Jennifer Appleton Gootman, "Features of Positive Youth Developmental Settings," *Prevention Researcher* 11, no. 2 (2004).

9. Joseph G. Kosciw and Elizabeth M. Diaz, *Involved, Invisible, Ignored: The Experiences of Lesbian, Gay, Bisexual, and Transgender Parents and Their Children in Our Nation's K–12 Schools* (New York: Gay, Lesbian, and Straight Education Network, 2008).

10. Tom Watkins, "Boy Scouts Tell Gay Leader to Take a Hike," CNN.com, October 19, 2010, http://articles.cnn.com/.

11. Ibid.

12. Personal communication, July 1, 2011.

13. Abigail Garner, *Families Like Mine: Children of Gay Parents Tell It Like It Is* (New York: Perennial Currents, 2004), 37.

14. Teresa LaFromboise et al., "Psychological Impact of Biculturalism: Evidence and Theory," *Psychological Bulletin* 114 (1993): 404.

15. Joseph G. Kosciw et al., *The 2009 National School Climate Survey: The Experiences of Lesbian, Gay, Bisexual and Transgender Students in Our Nation's Schools* (New York: Gay, Lesbian, and Straight Education Network, 2010).

16. Kosciw and Diaz, *Involved, Invisible, Ignored.*

17. Commission for Accreditation of Park and Recreation Agencies, *National Accreditation Standards* (Ashburn, VA: National Recreation and Park Association, 2009), v.

18. Ibid., 38.

19. GLSEN, "About the Project," http://sports.glsen.org/.

20. GLSEN, "Team Respect Challenge: Is Your Team Ready for the Team Respect Challenge?" http://sports.glsen.org/.

21. Frank Linnehan, Donna Chrobot-Mason, and Alison Konrad, "Diversity Attitudes and Norms: The Role of Ethnic Identity and Relational Demography," *Journal of Organizational Behavior* 27, no. 4 (2006).

Chapter 8: Religious Institutions

1. Rev. Winnie Varghese, HRC's Clergy Call 2011, available at http://www.hrc.org/.

2. Human Rights Campaign, "Stances of Faiths on LGBT Issues: American Baptist Church USA," http://www.hrc.org/.

3. Human Rights Campaign, "Stances of Faiths on LGBT Issues: Pentecostals," http://www.hrc.org/.

4. Human Rights Campaign, "Stances of Faiths on LGBT Issues: Roman Catholic Church," http://www.hrc.org/.

5. Ibid.

6. Thomas C. Fox, "Children Denied Catholic Schooling, Lesbian Couple Speaks Out," *National Catholic Reporter Online*, March 15, 2010, http://ncronline.org/.

7. Ibid.

8. Thomas C. Fox, "Boulder Pastor Says Jesus Turned Some Away," *National Catholic Reporter Online*, March 17, 2010, http://ncronline.org/.

9. Erica Meltzer, "Denver Archbishop Defends Sacred Heart of Jesus' Decision on Lesbians' Children at Boulder Preschool," DailyCamera.com, March 9, 2010.

10. Human Rights Campaign, "Roman Catholic Church."

11. *US Religious Landscape Survey* (Washington, DC: Pew Forum on Religion and Public Life, 2010).

12. Cited in Mark D. Jordan, *Recruiting Young Love* (Chicago: University of Chicago Press, 2011), 98.

13. *All in God's Family: Creating Allies for Our LGBT Families* (Minneapolis: National Gay and Lesbian Task Force's Institute for Welcoming Resources, 2009), 2.

14. Joe Kort, *Gay Affirmative Therapy for the Straight Clinician* (Norton: New York, 2008).

15. Sue Hyde, *Come Out and Win* (Boston: Beacon Press, 2007), 104.

16. DignityUSA, "What Is Dignity?" http://www.dignityusa.org/.

17. Jordan, *Recruiting Young Love*, 125.

18. DignityUSA, "Defying Gravity," http://voices.dignityusa.org/.

19. *Living Openly in Your Place of Worship* (Washington, DC: Human Rights Campaign, 2008).

20. Hyde, *Come Out and Win*, 127.

21. Ibid.

22. Rebecca Voelkel, *To Do Justice* (Minneapolis: National Gay and Lesbian Task Force's Institute for Welcoming Resources, 2009).

23. Ibid., 10.

24. Debra W. Haffner and Timothy Palmer, *Survey of Religious Progressives: A Report on Sexual Justice Advocacy in Progressive Faith Communities* (Westport, CT: Religious Institute on Sexual Morality, Justice, and Healing, 2009), http://www.religiousinstitute.org.

25. Ibid.

26. Denise Levy and Patricia Reeves, "Resolving Identity Conflict: Gay, Lesbian, and Queer Individuals with a Christian Upbringing," *Journal of Gay & Lesbian Social Services* 23 (2011).

27. *Living Openly in Your Place of Worship*, 4.

28. Believe Out Loud, "What Is Believe Out Loud?" http://www.believeoutloud.com/.

29. *All in God's Family: Creating Allies for Our LGBT Families* (Minneapolis: National Gay and Lesbian Task Force's Institute for Welcoming Resources, 2009), 2.

Chapter 9: The Legal System

1. NCAVP, *Hate Violence Against Lesbian, Gay, Bisexual, Transgender, Queer and HIV-Affected Communities in the United States in 2010* (New York: National Coalition of Anti-Violence Programs, 2011).

2. Ibid.

3. Sharon Stapel, personal communication, September 16, 2011.

4. Bianca D. M. Wilson, *Our Families: Attributes of Bay Area Lesbian, Gay, Bisexual & Transgender Parents and Their Children* (San Francisco: Our Family Coalition, 2007), 3.

5. National Gay and Lesbian Task Force Action Fund, "Overview: Task Force's Long History of Working to Secure Hate Crimes Protections for LGBT People," http://www.thetaskforce.org/.

6. Gregory M. Herek, "Hate Crimes and Stigma Related Experiences Among Sexual Minority Adults in the United States: Prevalence Estimates from a National Probability Sample," *Journal of Interpersonal Violence* 24, no. 1 (2009).

7. *A Guide to State-Level Advocacy Following Enactment of the Matthew Shepard and James Byrd, Jr. Hate Crimes Prevention Act* (Washington, DC: Human Rights Campaign, 2010).

8. Lynn Langton and Michael Planty, *Hate Crime 2003–2009* (Washington, DC: US Department of Justice, 2011).

9. Southern Poverty Law Center, "Government Survey: Hate Crimes Trending Downward," *Intelligence Report* 143 (2011): 11.

10. Queers for Economic Justice, *A Fabulous Attitude: Low-Income LGBTGNC People Surviving & Thriving on Love, Shelter, & Knowledge* (New York: Queers for Economic Justice, 2010).

11. NCAVP, *Hate Violence Against Lesbian, Gay, Bisexual, Transgender, Queer and HIV-Affected Communities.*

12. Personal communication, September 6, 2011.

13. *All Children Matter: How Legal and Social Inequalities Hurt LGBT Families* (Denver: Movement Advancement Project/Family Equality Council/Center for American Progress, October 2011).

14. NCAVP, *Anti-Lesbian, Gay, Bisexual, and Transgender Violence in 2007* (New York: National Coalition of Anti-Violence Programs, 2008), 42.

15. Amnesty International, *Stonewalled: Police Abuse and Misconduct Against Lesbian, Gay, Bisexual and Transgender People in the U.S.* (New York: Amnesty International, 2005).

16. US Department of Justice, Office of Justice Programs, Bureau of Justice Assistance, *A Policymaker's Guide to Hate Crimes* (Washington, DC: Government Printing Office, 1999), xii.

17. NCAVP, *Stories of LGBTQH Loss, Survival, & Resistance: Hate Violence Narratives from 2010* (New York: National Coalition of Anti-Violence Programs, 2011), 3.

18. Amnesty International, *Stonewalled.*

19. Ibid.

20. Ibid.

21. NCAVP, *Hate Violence Against Lesbian, Gay, Bisexual, Transgender, Queer and HIV-Affected Communities.*

22. Queers for Economic Justice, *A Fabulous Attitude.*

23. Joey L. Mogul, Andrea J. Ritchie, and Kay Whitlock, *Queer Injustice: The Criminalization of LGBT People in the United States* (Boston: Beacon Press, 2011), xviii.

24. NCAVP, *Hate Violence Against Lesbian, Gay, Bisexual, Transgender, Queer and HIV-Affected Communities.*

25. Sandhya Bathija, "Roy Moore 2.0?: An Ohio 'Commandments' Judge Would Like To Impose God's Law On You—And His Religious Right Mentors Are Even More Extreme," Americans United for Separation of Church and State, March 2010, http://www.au.org/.

26. *LeGaL Report on Sexual Orientation Fairness in Second Circuit Courts* (New York: LeGaL, 1997): 28.

27. New Jersey Supreme Court, *Final Report of the Task Force on Sexual Orientation Issues* (January 2, 2001), cited in Mogul et al., *Queer Injustice.*

28. Abbe Smith, "Homophobia in the Halls of Justice: Sexual Orientation Bias and Its Implications Within the Legal System: The Complex Uses of Sexual Orientation in Criminal Court," *Journal of Gender, Social Policy, & the Law* 11 (2003): 103–4.

29. *Why It Matters: Rethinking Victim Assistance for Lesbian, Gay, Bisexual, Transgender, and Queer Victims of Hate Violence & Intimate Partner Violence* (Washington, DC: National Center for Victims of Crime, 2010).

30. P. Tjaden and N. Thoennes, "Extent, Nature, and Consequences of Intimate Partner Violence: Findings from the National Violence Against Women Survey," US Department of Justice report NCJ 181867 (Washington, DC: Government Printing Office, 2000), http://www.ojp.usdoj.gov/.

31. G. L. Greenwood et al., "Battering Victimization Among a Probability-Based Sample of Men Who Have Sex with Men," *American Journal of Public Health* 92 (2002).

32. NCAVP, *Lesbian, Gay, Bisexual, Transgender, and Queer Domestic/Intimate Violence in the United States in 2009* (New York: National Coalition of Anti-Violence Programs, 2010).

33. *Why It Matters.*

34. Ibid.

35. Gregory M. Herek, J. Roy Gillis, and Jeanine C. Coogan, "Psychological Sequelae of Hate Crime Victimization among Lesbian, Gay, and Bisexual Adults," *Journal of Consulting and Clinical Psychology* 67, no. 6 (1999).

36. *Survival, Support, and Resilience: Stories of LGBTQ Survivors and Victims of Domestic/ Intimate Partner Violence* (New York: National Coalition of Anti-Violence Programs, 2010): 4.

37. Mogul, Ritchie, and Whitlock, *Queer Injustice.*

38. D'Anne Witkowski, "Creep of the Week: Bob Vander Plaats," *Philadelphia Gay News*, April 15, 2011.

39. BiasHELP, "Questions and Answers," http://www.biashelp.org/.

40. NCAVP, *Hate Violence Against Lesbian, Gay, Bisexual, Transgender, Queer and HIV-Affected Communities.*

41. Sylvia Rivera Law Project, "SRLP Opposes the Matthew Shepard and James Byrd, Jr. Hate Crimes Prevention Act," http://srlp.org/fedhatecrimelaw.

42. Personal communication, September 16, 2011.

Conclusion

1. James Scott, *Seeing Like a State: How Certain Schemes to Improve the Human Condition Have Failed* (New Haven, CT: Yale University Press, 1998), 138.

2. Scott E. Page, *The Difference: How the Power of Diversity Creates Better Groups, Firms, Schools, and Societies* (Princeton, NJ: Princeton University Press, 2007), 335.

3. *All Children Matter: How Legal and Social Inequalities Hurt LGBT Families* (Denver: Movement Advancement Project/Family Equality Council/Center for American Progress, October 2011).

4. Nancy Polikoff, *Beyond (Straight and Gay) Marriage* (Boston: Beacon Press, 2008), 210.

5. *All Children Matter*, 102.

6. Andrew Harmon, "Kerry, Nadler Propose Fair Housing Bill for LGBTs," *Advocate*, September 22, 2011, http://www.advocate.com/.

7. "10 Ways to Be an Ally & Friend," GLAAD, http://www.glaad.org/.

8. Gary J. Gates, "Family Formation and Raising Children Among Same-Sex Couples," *Family Focus on LGBT Families*, FF51 (2011): F2.

9. Ibid.

10. Personal communication, March 19, 2012.

11. David A. Fahrenthold, "'In God We Trust': House Reaffirms National Motto—Once Again," *Washington Post*, November 2, 2011, http://www.washingtonpost.com/.

12. Ibid.

Index